Mother of God
and our Mother

Mother of God and our Mother

An Introduction to Mariology

by ANTONIO OROZCO

Scepter Publishers
Princeton, NJ

Translated from *Madre de Dios y Madre Nuestra:*
Iniciación a la Mariología
© Ediciones Rialp, S.A.
Madrid, 1996

ISBN: 1–889334–00–6

Contents

Foreword

ORIGINALLY published in Madrid in 1996, *Madre de Dios y Madre Nuestra* is an introduction to Mariology designed to make accessible the rich heritage of the Church's understanding and love of the Blessed Virgin Mary. Its author, Father Antonio Orozco Delclós, holds a doctorate in scholastic philosophy from the Pontifical Lateran University in Rome. He also holds a licentiate in philosophy and letters from the University of Barcelona.

In the interests of accessibility, some adaptations have been made for this first English edition by its editor, Mary Gottschalk. Sources difficult if not impossible to obtain outside of Spain, for example, have been substituted by sources more readily available to English-speaking readers. In most instances, however, the authors are the same.

For the initial translation of the original, many thanks to Stephen Kane.

Introduction

THE CATHOLIC FAITH is Christocentric. Christ Jesus, Second Person of the Blessed Trinity, is the beginning and the end, the Alpha and the Omega, the great *pontifex,* or bridgemaker. Through his incarnation, life, passion, death, resurrection, and ascension into heaven Christ reestablished the union between God and the human race. He broke the chains that had kept us enslaved to our passions. Enslaved, that is, to passions disordered by sin; to Satan, who through sin exercises a certain power over the sinner; and to death, the most dramatic consequence of that rupture with God which sin is. At the same time, Christ earned for us an elevation (via participation) to divine life: a life replete with grace, with supernatural virtues, with gifts and fruits of the Holy Spirit; a life of much higher quality, of much deeper intimacy with God, than that enjoyed by our first parents in Eden. Our Lord Jesus Christ, in a way that no one could have dreamed of, has made us God's children and opened to us the gates of heaven. The Redemption is, then, not simply a rescue from the slavery of sin. It is justification; it is sanctification.

The divine mercy shines forth in the Incarnation of the Word and throughout his salvific work. Only Jesus Christ, perfect God and perfect man, is the perfect mediator between God and the human race. He alone is capable of uniting in his own person God and mankind. He is, in the radical sense of the term, the sole mediator. As Saint Paul says, "There is one God, and there is one mediator between God and men, the man Christ Jesus" (1 Tm 2:5). But Jesus is not a solitary mediator. Just as God, the one perfect Good (see Mt 19:17), allows all his creatures to participate in his goodness in various ways and degrees, so also Jesus gives mankind a real participation in his mediation. Certainly he is the one and only Redeemer. But it is no less certain that he wants every one of us to take an active part in his salvific work (see GS 22).

In a singular and sublime way, Christ Jesus chose to unite to his being and to his saving mission the Virgin Mary, who became his mother through the action of the Holy Spirit. He did this in such a profound way that it is impossible to comprehend properly the redemption accomplished by Christ without taking into account the active presence of the Blessed Virgin, his mother and ours (see LG 54). The Creator adorned her with extraordinary privileges, not the least of which is that, as Pope John Paul II said in Turin on April 13, 1980, she stood "by her Son's cross . . . courageously in solidarity with his suffering for us."[1]

In no way can Mary lead us away from Christ. On the contrary, as Pope John Paul also said in 1980, "no one in the history of the world has been more Christocentric and more Christophoric [Christ-bearing] than she. And no one has been more like him, not only with the natural likeness of mother and son, but with the likeness of the Spirit and holiness."[2]

God could have saved us in any number of ways. But the one that he chose—the Church has several strong reasons for believing this—was the best of all possible ways. He chose to take upon himself our human condition, excepting nothing but sin, and so be "born of a woman" (see Gal 4:4) whose response to her vocation was altogether positive and free, and who could therefore participate meritoriously in the entire length and breadth of the mystery of the redemption and sanctification of the human race.

But before we turn our focus to Mary, a word about Saint Joseph. He will be the focus of the last chapter of this book. If no one is more Christocentric than Mary, no one is more Marian than Saint Joseph. He was, as Saint Irenaeus expressed it, Mary's "predestined husband"[3]—the man chosen from all eternity to be the virginal spouse of the Mother of God. No Mariology would be complete without a section devoted to the one to whom the Blessed Trinity entrusted such an extraordinary role in the work of redemption.

1. "In the Cross God Changed the Meaning of Suffering": OR 4/28/80.

2. "Mary Chosen in Christ before the Creation": OR 12/15/80.

3. See O'Carroll 1983, 189.

1. Mary's Divine Motherhood

IN THE EASTERN PART of the Roman Empire there gradually arose among the Christian faithful the practice of addressing the Virgin Mary as *Theotokos*, or *Deipara*—Greek and Latin words meaning "God-bearing," or, more simply, "Mother of God." This expression, so appealing to many, was also for some a cause of concern. Even today, some non-Catholic theologians (strict followers of Calvin, for example) find it difficult to accept.[1]

Nestorius, a monk raised to the patriarchal see of Constantinople in 428, grew uneasy when he heard the Blessed Virgin acclaimed as *Theotokos*. It was not that he feared a revival of the ancient pagan mentality, long since rejected by Christians, which set up certain women as goddesses, or mothers of gods, through magical rites and sacred unions. There was nothing like this in the Christian world. Nestorius was not worried about picturesque imaginings associated with pagan fables. He was concerned with much deeper matters. The title *Theotokos* dealt a mortal blow to his Christology. For him, Christ had to have been a human subject united *to*, and therefore distinct from, the Word. He did not see it as even possible that the second divine Person could have taken on our human nature without there springing from the union two distinct subjects, or persons: one actually divine (the Son of God), the other merely human (Jesus of Nazareth).

What Nestorius in effect did was to divide Christ, by considering him a man (a most extraordinary one, to be sure) intimately united *to* God, but not himself truly God. Call Mary *Christotokos*, "Mother of Christ," the patriarch allowed, but never *Theotokos*.

At first glance, reason and prudence might appear to side with him. After all, how *could* a mere woman, a creature bounded by time, be the mother of the eternal Word of God—the Word proclaimed by the Council of Nicea, in the year 325, as "consubstantial" with

4

the Father? Nevertheless, the people of Constantinople, little as they understood about theological subtleties, replied that since she conceived and gave birth to the Word made flesh, to the Word who is God as truly as are the Father and the Holy Spirit, the Blessed Virgin Mary could and should be called Mother of God, *Theotokos.*

The uproar reached Alexandria and even Rome. Saints Cyril of Alexandria and Pope Celestine I confirmed the doctrine of faith professed and cherished by the faithful. And in order to definitively settle the question, the Council of Ephesus was convened, in 431.[2]

Toward understanding the mystery

But before considering the magisterium's definitions on the mysteries of Christ's being and Mary's divine motherhood, we need to clarify two concepts essential to any understanding of these two mysteries: namely, the concepts of "nature" and "person."

That Mary should be the Mother of God involves another great mystery, perhaps the one most difficult for the human mind to penetrate: the incarnation of the Word. That the Word of God, the Second Person of the Blessed Trinity, took upon himself a human nature, a nature formed in the womb of the Virgin Mary, such that the person conceived is truly human (since the created nature he assumed and possesses is truly human) without ceasing to be God—this mystery infinitely transcends our human reason; we will never come close to completely understanding it. Nevertheless, it is not opposed to the light of our intellect and is therefore, to a certain extent, intelligible.

Nature and person

During those third- and fourth-century controversies on the mystery of the God-Man, the Church began to use two terms that are usually translated as "nature" and "person," respectively. These are not synonymous terms. They designate really distinct principles, even though, as a matter of fact, every instance of human nature is accompanied by personhood, and every person (human) has a nature (human). The fact that language so consistently reflects the distinction confirms that it is not a semantic fabrication. Indeed, it is not the same thing to use the word "what" when asking a question as it is to use the word "who."

"What are you?" If you asked me that question, I would answer: "I'm a man. I'm a male individual of the human species. I have a human nature; I'm human." But if you asked me, "*Who* are you?" I would answer: "I'm Father Antonio Orozco."

Strictly speaking, "I" am not first and foremost a "what"; "I" am basically a "who." I am not some*thing*; I am someo*ne*. Or, to be more precise, I *have* a nature, but I *am* a person.

The relevant metaphysical considerations would unnecessarily complicate our discussion. Surely it is easy enough to understand that a "what" is not the same as a "who"; that "nature" and "person" are quite different realities.

This distinction is absolutely necessary for understanding that it is not absurd or impossible for a human nature to belong to a non-human person.

The subject of any individual human nature is necessarily a person. The contrary is inconceivable. But it is conceivable that God could (and we know from revelation that he did) create a human nature such that the "I" underlying this nature, the subject possessing it, is a divine "I"; that is, one of the Persons of the Blessed Trinity. This is truly an unfathomable mystery. Never could we have imagined that God—the one, transcendent Creator—would even want to do such a thing. But it does not contradict reason. Yes, it would be contradictory for a human nature to become divine, or vice versa, and we would be running right into that contradiction if "nature" and "person" were synonymous terms. However, it is not contradictory for a divine Person, without ceasing to be divine, to take on a human nature and become himself the subject of this humanity.

The Catholic Church teaches that God, when he took on a human nature in the immaculate womb of Mary, became the subject of the human being conceived in Mary by the power of the Holy Spirit (see ND 604–608, 644). From the moment the Blessed Virgin uttered her *fiat,* the Word could say: "I am this human being." Jesus, engendered by the operation of the Holy Spirit, is truly human, since he has a real, flesh-and-blood human nature. At the same time, he is truly divine, since the person who sustains this nature is God the Son. In a mysterious fashion, the eternal Word of God becomes one of us: an individual with a nature exactly like yours and mine (except for sin), but one with a unique individuality. This man is the Word. The "I" of this man, Jesus, is the divine "I" of God the Son.

The person is neither the body nor the soul, nor the body and soul combined. Body and soul make up human nature; they make a human being whole and complete. But a person is more than a complete human entity. A person is an irreducible, independent, and autonomous subject, of whom we predicate generation, conception, birth, filiation. In this sense, the "subject" of Jesus (or, more exactly, the "subject" *called* Jesus—the son of Mary) is truly God the Son.

In Christ, then, *there is no human person.* But he has, nevertheless, a complete human nature, with all the perfections a human nature can possess. This nature is sustained, actualized, and vivified by a particular person: the Second Person of the Blessed Trinity. Mary conceived, by the power of the Holy Spirit, a real human being who from the first moment of his existence was really God.

Mary is clearly the mother of the man Jesus, since she gave him everything that any mother gives her son. But we must add immediately that the "who" of Jesus is the Second Person of the Blessed Trinity. Every true mother is the mother of her entire child, both nature and person. This is only logical, since nature and person are distinct but not *separable* realities. Hence, Mary is truly and rightly called Mother of God, because she conceived the human nature of Jesus, whose person is divine. I'll say it again:

Mary gave Jesus, who is God the Son, everything any mother gives her child. She therefore is, beyond the shadow of a doubt, in the most strictly proper sense of the term, Mother of God the Son. This explanation accords perfectly with the Catholic formulation of the dogma, defined in 431 by the General Council of Ephesus in response to the errors of Nestorius. "The holy Virgin," declared the Council, "is the Mother of God (*Theotokos*), since she begot according to the flesh the Word of God made flesh" (ND 606/1). In 451 the General Council of Chalcedon proclaimed that Christ "was born as to His humanity from Mary the Virgin Mother of God" (ND 614). And in 553 the Second General Council of Constantinople added the clarification that the "ever virgin" Mary is the "Mother of God" not "by an abuse of language," but, rather, "in the true sense" (ND 620/6).

Throughout the history of the Church, the magisterium has continually confronted various errors concerning the mystery of Mary, Mother of God. Among other truths, the Church has affirmed these:

• "The Son of God . . . worked with human hands, he thought with a human mind. He acted with a human will, and with a human heart he loved. Born of the Virgin Mary, he has truly been made one of us, like us in all things except sin" (GS 22).

• It is not the case that "the Son of God took nothing from his virgin mother but [instead] assumed a heavenly body and passed through the virgin's womb like water flowing down an aqueduct."[3]

• What we assert by calling Mary "Mother of God" is not "that the nature of the Word or His divinity received the beginning of its existence from the holy Virgin, but that, since the holy body, animated by a rational soul, which the Word united to Himself hypostatically (*kath' hupostasin*), was born from her, the Word was born according to the flesh."[4]

In the introduction to chapter eight of *Lumen Gentium*, the Second Vatican Council, reiterating the constant teaching of the

Church, made this statement: "The Virgin Mary, who at the message of the angel received the Word of God in her heart and in her body and gave Life to the world, is acknowledged and honored as being truly the Mother of God and Mother of the Redeemer" (LG 53). Pope John Paul II is tireless in calling to mind, for the joy and encouragement of all the faithful, this great mystery (see, for example, RM 4).

Sacred Scripture

Though not with the clarity of the New Testament, the Old Testament contains references to the mystery we are now studying. The *Catechism of the Catholic Church* (no. 489) gives this overview:

> Throughout the Old Covenant the mission of many holy women *prepared* for that of Mary. At the very beginning there was Eve; despite her disobedience, she receives the promise of a posterity that will be victorious over the evil one, as well as the promise that she will be the mother of all the living (cf. Gn 3:15, 20). By virtue of this promise, Sarah conceives a son in spite of her old age (cf. Gn 18:10–14; 21:1–2). Against all human expectation God chooses those who were considered powerless and weak to show forth his faithfulness to his promises: Hannah, the mother of Samuel; Deborah; Ruth; Judith and Esther; and many other women (cf. 1 Cor 1:17; 1 Sm 1). Mary "stands out among the poor and humble of the Lord, who confidently hope for and receive salvation from him. After a long period of waiting the times are fulfilled in her, . . . and the new plan of salvation is established" (LG 55).

There also appears in the Old Testament a figure called the *gebirah*: the mother of the king, the queen mother, who possesses great dignity and power.[5] Solomon, for example, honors his mother, Bathsheba, by placing her at his right hand when he sits on his throne (see 1 Kgs 2:19). In Matthew 2:11 and Luke 1:30–33 we see reflections of that image. Finally, various prophets speak of the "Daughter of Zion," who represents the mystery of Israel's simultaneous identity as virgin, spouse, and mother.[6] In the New Testament the divine motherhood of Mary is *implicitly* affirmed wherever she is referred to as "the mother of Jesus," since Jesus clearly identified himself as God (see Jn 8:58 and 10:30). His enemies understood that identification so well that they took it as blasphemy, a justification for crucifying him (see Jn 10:31–33). The earliest text is Galatians 4:4, where Saint Paul mentions Mary without naming her. He says: "God sent forth his Son, born of woman. . . ." Actually he says "*made of a* woman"—a remarkable choice of words indicating clearly, as Tertullian pointed out, "that the Word was made flesh and that that flesh was truly taken from the Blessed Virgin."[7] Mark calls Jesus "Son of God" (1:1) and "son of Mary" (6:3). In Matthew (chapters 1 and 2) and Luke (chapters 1 and 2) the word "mother," or a descriptive equivalent of it, is used with reference to the conception and birth of Christ. The angel Gabriel tells Mary: "You will conceive in your womb and bear a son, and you shall call his name Jesus" (Lk 1:31). As for John, not once in his Gospel does he call her "Mary." Just as he never refers to himself by name, this "disciple whom Jesus loved" consistently refers to her as "the mother of Jesus."[8]

The New Testament also *explicitly* teaches the mystery of the divine motherhood of Mary. Gabriel says to her: "The Holy Spirit will come upon you, and the power of the Most High will overshadow you; therefore the child to be born will be called holy, the Son of God" (Lk 1:35). The son of Mary will be called "Emmanuel . . . God with us" (Mt 1:23). The angel tells Joseph (Mt 1:21) that Jesus "will save his people": an expression which in the Old Testament is reserved for God (see Is 49:25; Jer 15:20–21; Ez 13:21; Zec 8:7). Moreover, Jesus "will save his people *from their sins*": a feat that only God can accomplish (see Ps 130:8 and Mk 2:5–7). Moved by the Holy Spirit, Elizabeth asks Mary: "Why is this granted me, that the mother of my Lord [*kyrios*] should come to me?" (Lk 1:43). The Jews called God "Lord." As Father John McKenzie points out, "it is not without significance that the use of the word *kyrios* in the Septuagint is the usual divine name" (1965, 518).

Sacred Tradition

The early Fathers of the Church, including Saint Ignatius of Antioch (d. *c.* 110), Saint Justin Martyr (d. *c.* 165), Saint Irenaeus (d. *c.* 202), Tertullian (d. after 220), and Saint Hippolytus of Rome (d. 235), all make reference to Mary's motherhood.[9] As for *Theotokos,* Father Michael O'Carroll (1983, 342) tells us this: "The first certain literary use of the title is attributed to Alexander of Alexandria in 325. Thereafter it is found widely, especially with Saint Athanasius and the Alexandrians, in Palestine with Eusebius of Caeserea and Cyril of Jerusalem, with the three Cappadocians, with Eustathius of Antioch and the Council of Antioch in 341, Apollinarius of Laodicea, Diodorus of Tarsus, Severian of Gabala— even Arians like Asterius the Sophist used it."[10] "Saint Ambrose first used the title *Mater Dei* in the West. In the next century, Saint Cyril of Alexandria brought the question to a church council, which decided to answer in his very terms. The fullest exposition of the theology of the divine motherhood in the patristic period was made by Saint John of Damascus" (O'Carroll 1983, 258).

The dignity of the Mother of God

"The humanity of Christ," says Saint Thomas Aquinas, "from the fact that it is united to the Godhead; and created happiness from the fact that it is the fruition of God; and the Blessed Virgin from the fact that she is the Mother of God; have all a certain infinite dignity from the infinite good, which is God" (ST I.25.6.4). Mary is the only one besides God the Father who can with literal accuracy say to God the Son: "You are my son." "To the Blessed Virgin alone is due the cult of hyperdulia," says Cajetan, "because she alone by her own natural operation has approached the limits of the Deity, conceiving and giving birth to God and nourishing Him with her milk." [11]

Certainly there is a danger of going too far in proclaiming Mary's sublime dignity. The Second Vatican Council, well aware of this danger, urged "theologians and preachers of the divine word to abstain zealously both from all gross exaggerations as well as from petty narrow-mindedness in considering the singular dignity of the Mother of God" (LG 67).

It would be a terrible aberration to consider the Blessed Virgin a being clothed in divine dignity without connecting this marvelous reality with the Persons to whom she herself knows she owes absolutely everything that she is: namely, God the Father, God the Son, and God the Holy Spirit. Mary's divine motherhood is an altogether gratuitous supernatural gift. Mary sees herself as "the handmaid of the Lord"; she knows full well that she owes all her dignity to her Creator, her Redeemer, and her Sanctifier. Yet it is no exaggeration to call her, as did Saint Lawrence of Brindisi, "the daughter of God the Father, the true Mother of God the Son, the spouse and unique comfort of the Holy Spirit, the Queen of heaven, the mistress of angels, the empress of the universe." [12]

Daughter of God the Father, Mother of God the Son, Spouse of God the Holy Spirit

Indeed, declares Father Cyril Papali, "the Church loves to address her as the Daughter of God the Father, the Mother of God the Son, the Spouse of God the Holy Ghost." [13] The Second Vatican Council proclaimed that Mary "is endowed with the high office and dignity of being the Mother of the Son of God, by which account she is also the beloved daughter of the Father and the temple of the Holy Spirit" (LG 53), and Pope John Paul has reiterated this statement (in RM 9).

Granted, the Second Vatican Council refrained from using the expression "spouse of the Holy Spirit," possibly because it is open to misinterpretation, and possibly because there is also theological reason to call Mary the spouse of the Father, and even the spouse of Christ.[14] Certainly Mary is not the spouse of the Holy Spirit in the same sense that husbands and wives are spouses to one another. In the first place, she is not divine, and in the second place she was married to Saint Joseph! Nevertheless, as Pope John Paul expresses it, "the Holy Spirit, who had already infused the fullness of grace into Mary of Nazareth, formed in her virginal womb the human nature of Christ" (RM 1). In some real sense, then, there is a spousal relationship between Mary and the Holy Spirit. Thus Pope Paul VI, in section 26 of his apostolic exhortation *Marialis Cultus,* quotes approvingly the assertion of Prudentius that "the unwed Virgin espoused the Spirit," and Pope John Paul likewise states that at the Annunciation "she became his faithful spouse" (RM 26).

Seat of all graces

Mary was predestined, says Pope John Paul, not only to be the Mother of God, but to be the *worthy* Mother of God.[15] In accord with divine logic, Mary's heart, filled with grace, harbored a love above all others, so that she would have for her Son sentiments proper to the Mother of the God-Man.

In *The Three Greatest Prayers: Commentaries on the Lord's Prayer, the Hail Mary, and the Apostles' Creed* (1990, 165–68), Saint Thomas Aquinas distinguishes three basic aspects of Mary's fullness of grace:

• "*Grace filled her soul. . . .* Thus it is said: 'Thou art all fair, O my love; and there is not a spot in thee.' . . . She practiced the works of *all* the virtues, while other saints were conspicuous in certain particular virtues. . . . The Blessed Virgin was full of grace both in performing good works and in avoiding evil deeds.

• *"Grace overflowed into her body.* . . . The Blessed Virgin was so full of grace that it overflowed into her flesh, fitting it for the conception of God's Son. Thus Hugh of St. Victor says, 'The Holy Ghost had so kindled in her heart the fire of divine love that it worked wonders in her flesh, yea, even so that she gave birth to God made man.'

• *"Grace overflows from her onto all mankind.* . . . It is, indeed, a great thing that any one saint has so much grace that it is conducive to the salvation of many; but it is most wondrous to have so much grace as to suffice for the salvation of all mankind. Thus it is in Christ and [in a derivative way] in the Blessed Virgin."

The mystery of the woman "Full of Grace" brings us to the subject we are going to study next: the Immaculate Conception of the Mother of God.

1. See O'Carroll 1983, 94.
2. See LV: PDM, 158–75; Kelly 1960, 310–17; O'Carroll 1983, 111–14; Papali 1987, 44–47.
3. Council of Florence, apostolic constitution *Cantate Domino*: CIN.
4. Council of Ephesus, "Second Letter of Cyril of Alexandria to Nestorius": ND 605.
5. See McKenzie 1965, 709.
6. See La 2:13; Is 62:4–5, 11–12; Jer 4:31; see also de la Potterie 1992, xxiv–xl.
7. See Papali 1987, 39–40.
8. Papali 1987, 46; see Jn 2:1–12 and 19:25–27.
9. See FEF 1:42, 141, 223, 277, 394.
10. See also O'Carroll 1983, 257–58, and FEF 1:680, 788, 824; 2:1017, 1020a.
11. *In IIam IIae*, q. 103, a. 4: Llamera 1962, 150–51.

12. See O'Carroll 1983, 216.
13. Papali 1987, 32; see also Roschini 1962, 34, and Escrivá, *The Way*: 496.
14. See O'Carroll 1983, 333.
15. See Angelus Message of December 8, 1983; Brown 1990, 96.

2. The Immaculate Conception

AMONG THE PRIVILEGES God granted the Blessed Virgin in accord with her lofty dignity as the Mother of God and in virtue of the merits of her Son, the most outstanding is her Immaculate Conception. Always implicitly affirmed by the Church, it was defined as a dogma of faith by Pope Pius IX on December 8, 1854, in the apostolic constitution *Ineffabilis Deus*. In issuing this decree, he was, as Pope Pius XII would later phrase it, "merely carefully conserving and sanctioning with his authority the teaching of the Fathers and of the whole Church from its earliest days down through the centuries."[1]

The text of the definition runs as follows: "We declare, pronounce, and define that the doctrine which holds that the most Blessed Virgin Mary, in the first instant of her conception, by a singular grace and privilege granted by Almighty God, in view of the merits of Jesus Christ, the Savior of the human race, was preserved free from all stain of original sin, is a doctrine revealed by God and therefore to be believed firmly and constantly by all the faithful."[2] Clearly the dogma refers not to Christ's virginal conception in Mary by the work of the Holy Spirit, but to Mary's own conception in her mother's womb. Clearly, too, it refers not to the "active" conception, the work of Mary's parents, but to its end or outcome, the "passive" conception: the beginning of her life. At this moment it is Mary, and only Mary, who is without original sin. She is conceived free of all sin, and so she shall remain.

During the Middle Ages some highly respectable theologians, including Saint Thomas Aquinas, maintained that the Blessed Virgin contracted original sin only for a moment and then was immediately sanctified by God in her mother's womb.[3] Their conviction was based partially on a faulty understanding of biology, but primarily on some as yet unresolved theological difficulties. In any event, *Ineffabilis Deus* definitely excluded any such theory.

With the phrase "preserved free from all stain of original sin," the Church professes that Mary was never at any moment or in any way affected by original sin—that sin transmitted by generation from the time of our first parents. As Pope Pius XII says, when it comes to Mary "the question of sin does not even arise" (FCor: PDM, 255). Quoting Cornelius à Lapide, he declares that "'she is the purest and the most holy, so that under God a greater purity cannot be understood'" (FCor: PDM, 256).

Mary's freedom from sin is a "singular grace and privilege" from Almighty God. Might there be another exception? Nowhere in *Ineffabilis Deus* does Pope Pius IX either affirm the possibility or definitively rule it out. However, Pope Pius XII, in *Fulgens Corona,* does state that Mary "obtained this singular privilege, *never granted to anyone else,* because she was raised to the dignity of Mother of God."[4]

Apostolic Tradition and the magisterium

The truth of the Immaculate Conception was not deduced, either from revelation in general or from a connection with another revealed truth. Rather, it is a truth formally revealed by God and affirmed by the Church throughout her existence. Over the course of history, however, there has been progress in understanding and explaining this truth (cf. CCC 491).

Only during the scholastic period did theologians begin serious discussion of the Immaculate Conception. But Pope Sixtus IV approved a feast day and a divine office in 1476 and 1483, respectively.[5] He also prohibited "all censure of the belief in the Immaculate Conception, while at the same time he forbade making the denial of it a heresy" (Scheeben 2:34). In 1708 Pope Clement XI made the feast day a holy day of obligation for the universal Church (Kelly 1986, 292).

Resolving theological difficulties

What were the problems that, previous to the dogmatic definition, still kept some theologians from recognizing the truth of the

Immaculate Conception? Basically they boiled down to one: Does it not clash with the truth of the universal redemption wrought by Christ? How can Mary be an exception to the inheritance of original sin, and therefore to the need for redemption?

The response of the magisterium is this: Mary was not exempt from the need for redemption. Far to the contrary, she "was redeemed from the moment of her conception" (CCC 491). The dogmatic definition itself clearly states that her preservation "from all stain of original sin" was granted by God "in view of the merits of Jesus Christ, the Savior of the human race." That is how it came to be that she was "adorned from the first instant of her conception with the radiance of an entirely unique holiness" (LG 56).

But how can a person be redeemed without ever having contracted original sin? It was John Duns Scotus who provided the solution to this problem, with his distinction between "liberative" and "preservative" redemption.[6] The former is applied to the rest of us by our "washing of regeneration" in the waters of baptism (see Ti 3:5); the latter occurred in Mary before she could even incur the stain of original sin.

Actually, as Duns Scotus pointed out, Mary more than anyone else needed Christ as redeemer, "for as others needed Christ so that through his merit they should be forgiven sin already contracted, so she needed the mediator preserving from sin (*praeveniente peccatum*) lest she should ever have to contract it or should contract it."[7]

In *Ineffabilis Deus* Pope Pius IX expressed all this with the utmost clarity. "By virtue of the foreseen merits of Christ, our Lord and Redeemer," he said, Mary "was never subject to original sin, but was completely preserved from the original taint, and hence she was redeemed in a manner more sublime."[8]

Sacred Scripture

The Church has found in Sacred Scripture a solid foundation for the doctrine of the Immaculate Conception. Several Church Fathers, Doctors, and other authorized interpreters have perceived as referring to the Blessed Virgin these words spoken by God to the serpent after the Fall: "I will put enmity between you and the woman, and between your seed and her seed . . ." (Gn 3:15). This is the famous *protoevangelium,* the first announcement—made immediately after the first sin—of the good news (= gospel) of the future redemption. "Seed" (posterity) is interpreted not only in a collective and moral sense, but also in a specifically Christological and Mariological sense. The verse expresses the enmity between, on the one side, Satan and his followers, and, on the other side, Christ the Redeemer and Mary his mother.

As Pope Pius IX noted (ID, p. 14), the Fathers of the Church based their conviction of Mary's unblemished holiness on what was said to her at the Annunciation. "When [they] meditated on the fact that the most Blessed Virgin was, in the name and by order of God himself, proclaimed full of grace by the angel Gabriel when he announced her most sublime dignity of Mother of God, they thought that this singular and solemn salutation, never heard before, showed that the Mother of God is the seat of all divine graces and is adorned with all gifts of the Holy Spirit. To them Mary is an almost infinite treasury, an inexhaustible abyss of these gifts, to such an extent that she was never subject to the curse and was, together with her Son, the only partaker of perpetual benediction. Hence she was worthy to hear Elizabeth, inspired by the Holy Spirit, exclaim: 'Blessed are you among women, and blessed is the fruit of your womb.'"

So, too, they concluded that Mary is the New Eve. "Eve, a virgin and undefiled," said Saint Justin Martyr, "conceived the word of the serpent, and bore disobedience and death. But the Virgin Mary received faith and joy when the angel Gabriel announced to her the glad tidings that the Spirit of the Lord would come upon her and the power of the Most High would overshadow her, for which reason the Holy One being born of her is the Son of God. And she replied: 'Be it done unto me according to thy word'" (FEF 1:141). "The knot of Eve's disobedience," said Saint Irenaeus, "was loosed by the obedience of Mary. What the virgin Eve had bound in unbelief, the Virgin Mary loosed through faith" (FEF 1:224).

The Mariological interpretation of the protoevangelium is, by the way, independent of the controversy concerning proper translation of this text. The Hebrew text, at least the oldest one extant, does properly translate as "*he* shall bruise your head," and the Septuagint agrees with the Hebrew.[9] However, "the biblical argument for the Immaculate Conception of the Blessed Virgin is not taken from the expression 'she shall crush thy head,' but from the implacable 'enmity' between the woman and Satan" (Parente 1951, 233).[10] Father Joseph Pohle (1948, 44–45) explains this in detail:

> According to the well nigh unanimous interpretation of the Fathers, beginning with Saint Justin Martyr and Saint Ignatius of Antioch, the "serpent crusher" is a determinate person, namely our Divine Savior Jesus Christ Himself, and the woman whose enmity is destined to prove fatal to the serpent is the Blessed Virgin Mary. These two persons are opposed to two other beings, namely, the serpent, who is none other than Satan, and his "seed," i.e., his clientele of sinners. God Himself has "put enmity" between these two pairs, Christ and His mother on the one side, and Satan and his followers on the other—an enmity which will ultimately end in victory for the former and destruction for the latter. Mary, being on the side of Christ, with the same enmity between her and Satan as that which exists between the latter and her Divine Son, must also share in His triumph. This would not be the case had she, even for a single moment, been tainted by original sin; for in that hypothesis Satan would have triumphed over her, and she would have been, at least temporarily, his friend and ally, and the Protogospel would consequently be untrue. It follows that, viewed in the light of Christian tradition, the Protoevangelium foreshadows not only the victory achieved by Christ through the atonement, but implicitly also the Immaculate Conception of His Blessed Mother.

The Immaculate Conception is foreshadowed in many other Old Testament images as well. In *Ineffabilis Deus* (pp. 13–14) Pope

Pius IX gives us a beautiful overview: "This sublime and singular privilege of the Blessed Virgin, together with her most excellent innocence, purity, holiness and freedom from every stain of sin, as well as the unspeakable abundance and greatness of all heavenly graces, virtues and privileges—these the Fathers beheld in that ark of Noah, which was built by divine command and escaped entirely safe and sound from the common shipwreck of the whole world (cf. Gn 6:9); in the ladder which Jacob saw reaching from the earth to heaven, by whose rungs the angels of God ascended and descended, and on whose top the Lord himself leaned (cf. Gn 28:12); in that bush which Moses saw in the holy place burning on all sides, which was not consumed or injured in any way but grew green and blossomed beautifully (cf. Ex 3:2); in that impregnable tower before the enemy, from which hung a thousand bucklers and all the armor of the strong (cf. Sg 4:4); in that garden enclosed on all sides, which cannot be violated or corrupted by any deceitful plots (cf. Sg 4:12); as in that resplendent city of God, which has its foundations on the holy mountains (cf. Ps 87:1); in that most august temple of God, which, radiant with divine splendors, is full of the glory of God (cf. Is 6:1–4); and in very many other biblical types of this kind."

Divine reasons

The Church never defines a dogma on arbitrary or aesthetic grounds. She always exercises her authority on the grounds of sound reason, Sacred Scripture, apostolic tradition, and the sense of the faithful. The mystery that we are now studying is no exception.

The underlying principles that the Church has found for God's design regarding the Immaculate Conception are these:

• *Mary's divine motherhood.* Mary "was enriched by God with the gifts which befit such a role" (LG 56). Indeed, the "high office" of being the Mother of God "*demands* the fullness of divine grace and a soul immune from stain, since it requires the greatest dignity and sanctity after Christ."[11]

- *God's love for his mother.* As Blessed Josemaría says, "We face here a mystery of love. . . . How would we have acted, if we could have chosen our own mother? I'm sure we would have chosen the one we have, adorning her with every possible grace. That is what Christ did. Being all-powerful, all-wise, Love itself (cf. 1 Jn 4:8), his power carried out his will. . . . [Duns Scotus] put it this way: 'It was fitting; God could do so; therefore he did.'"[12]

- *Mary's need for unimpaired freedom.* "In order for Mary to be able to give the free assent of her faith to the announcement of her vocation, it was necessary that she be wholly borne by God's grace" (CCC 490). This point calls for special consideration. Mary's response to the angel's message from God required all the strength of the *purest freedom*: a freedom open to receiving the greatest gift imaginable, but also to accepting the heaviest cross ever placed on any mother's heart. For the Blessed Virgin, whose soul was filled with the most exquisite love, accepting the will of God meant having that soul pierced with a sword of unspeakable sorrow (see Lk 2:35). It was unimaginably hard for her to accept such a destiny as scourging, ridicule, and crucifixion for the One she loved so much more than herself. The Blessed Virgin needed all the strength of her human will and the fullness of the infused virtues and gifts of the Holy Spirit to freely give her emphatic *yes* to God's plan. Her immense spiritual wealth does not diminish her merit; it simply makes possible in a splendid way what would otherwise have been impossible. It gives Mary the capacity to say a wholehearted, unconditional, entirely free yes to God. Likewise, God gives me the grace to say yes to my divine vocation; without that grace, I could never say yes. But with it, I am not forced to say yes; I could say no. A divine vocation is not a command, it's an invitation. Along with the "Come, follow me" is an implied "if you want to" (see Mk 10:21 and Jn 21:15–19).

Privileges included in Mary's fullness of grace

The mystery of Mary's fullness of grace is a beauty of spectacular depth. Among its rich dimensions are these:

- *Freedom from the slightest taint of sin.* "Mary benefited first of all and uniquely from Christ's victory over sin: she was preserved from all stain of original sin and by a special grace of God committed no sin of any kind during her whole earthly life" (CCC 411). "God's grace so encompassed her that never once did she offend God by the slightest venial imperfection. Even those daily faults and failings from which no human creature in God's ordinary Providence can be exempt, even from these the Mother of God . . . was preserved perpetually immune . . ." (Smith 1938, 50–51).

- *Freedom from any attraction to evil.* "The Blessed Virgin was neither metaphysically nor physically impeccable and therefore the real possibility of sinning was left to her. But *morally* sin was impossible to her" (Friethoff 1958, 92). She enjoyed a "freedom from all the effects of original sin which, in one way or another, belong to the moral domain, i.e., from all inclination to sin, and in general, from all irregularity connected in the soul with the positive safeguarding against each, even the smallest, personal sin" (Scheeben 2:29).

- *Fullness of virtue.* Mary "had all virtues most perfectly" (St. Bonaventure, O'Carroll, 84). "That our Lady practiced all virtues in a most excellent manner at all times is a thesis now universally received among Catholic theologians" (Carol 1956, 129).

- *An ongoing increase of grace.* "As the light of dawn differs from the full light of day, so Mary's fullness of grace differs from that of Christ insofar as it was not complete from the beginning but was subject to an interior progress" (Scheeben 2:12). Mary's initial fullness of grace was not absolute and infinite like that of Christ; of all human beings, he is the only one united hypostatically with the Word. Her fullness of grace was relative: perfect, but not infinite. If Jesus "increased in wisdom and in stature, and in favor with God and man" (Lk 2:52), it is certainly true that Mary, too, could and did grow in grace.

After all, as George Smith points out, "the characteristic activity of grace is charity, and in the love of God the soul of Mary was incessantly active. Thus all her actions, most pleasing in the sight of

God, animated as they were every one by the most ardent charity, must have merited for her a continual increase in grace. . . . Truly Mary was full of grace, full of grace not in the sense that nothing could be added to it, but full in the sense that there was never a moment in her life when she did not comply perfectly with God's will, thus increasing daily her capacity to receive further outpourings of the divine life into her soul" (1938, 51–52).

Theologians commonly hold that at the moment of the Incarnation, Mary received an abundant increase in grace in consequence of her *yes*. Saint Thomas, for example, teaches that there was in her "a threefold perfection of grace. . . . The second perfection of grace in the Blessed Virgin was through the presence of the Son of God Incarnate in her womb" (ST III.27.5.2). This is perfectly logical if we consider Christ the Man as cause of grace, subordinate only to the First Cause, namely, God. Furthermore, the reciprocal love between the Son and his mother must surely have been the cause of an uninterrupted increase of grace for the mother.

Nevertheless, it is quite certain that Mary suffered grievously on account of her participation "in the death of her Son, in his redeeming death" (RM 18). Far from exempting her from suffering, her Immaculate Conception actually increased her capacity for it. It disposed her to take advantage of the sufferings permitted by God the Father and, in cooperation with her Son, to offer her sufferings with his for our salvation. Pope John Paul makes the connection crystal-clear: "She advanced in her pilgrimage of faith, and in this *pilgrimage* to the foot of the cross there was simultaneously accomplished her maternal *cooperation* with the Savior's whole mission through her actions and sufferings. Along the path of this collaboration with the work of her Son, the Redeemer, Mary's motherhood itself underwent a singular transformation, becoming ever more imbued with 'burning charity' toward all those to whom Christ's mission was directed. Through this 'burning charity,' which sought to achieve, in union with Christ, the restoration of 'supernatural life to souls,' Mary *entered, in a way all her own, into the one mediation* 'between God and men' *which is the mediation of the man Christ Jesus*. If she was the first to experience

within herself the supernatural consequences of this one mediation—in the Annunciation she had been greeted as 'full of
grace'—then we must say that through this fullness of grace and
supernatural life she was especially predisposed to cooperation
with Christ, the one Mediator of human salvation" (RM 39).

This most highly exalted creature is not, however, the one far-
thest removed from our littleness. The Second Vatican Council,
wishing to eradicate any misunderstanding on that point, stated
emphatically that Mary's place in the Church "is the highest after
Christ and yet very close to us" (LG 54).

1. FCor: PDM, 254.
2. St. Paul edition, p. 21.
3. See ST III.27.1–6 and the introduction to that section; see
    also Scheeben 2:83–111, and Papali 1987, 21–23.
4. PDM, 255; emphasis added.
5. See Kelly 1986, 250, and Scheeben 2:34.
6. See O'Carroll 1983, 307, 320–21.
7. O'Carroll 1983, 321; see also Papali 1987, 22–23.
8. St. Paul edition, p. 11.
9. See Pohle 1948, 43.
10. See also FCor: PDM, 254.
11. FCor: PDM, 255–56; emphasis added.
12. Escrivá, *Christ Is Passing By*, 171.

3. The Virginity of Mary

THESE MYSTERIES of faith are divinely interrelated: the mystery of the Blessed Trinity, the mystery of the Incarnation of the Word, the mystery of Mary's human and divine motherhood. She is the Mother of God from the time she says her *fiat* concerning the Emmanuel, the "God with us." The Son begotten of the Father through all eternity is conceived by Mary by the power of the Holy Spirit, with the result that perfect God becomes, forever after, perfect man as well.

Mary's divine motherhood is the principal and greatest mystery of her person. She was conceived without any stain of sin, filled with grace, and called to perpetual virginity, all in view of this immense miracle that would be carried out years later. Motherhood and virginity are by nature mutually exclusive realities, but God chose to miraculously unite them in his mother.

For those who do not believe in an all-powerful God, it is logical not to believe that this could happen, that a woman could be simultaneously a virgin and a mother. Actually, though, this should not be a stumbling block for anyone, since it is illogical to believe either that God does not exist at all or that he is not the free and all-powerful Creator of everything there is.

Let us keep in mind that the Catholic faith definitely affirms Mary's bodily virginity. Her spiritual virginity (her unswerving fidelity, her uncompromised holiness), also affirmed by the Church, is amazing enough. But her physical virginity is more obviously problematic. The Church has, after all, always affirmed that Mary is the mother of Jesus in the ordinary, material sense. "She conceived in true reality without human seed from the Holy Spirit, God the Word Himself, who before the ages was born of God the Father."[1]

The creed we pray at Mass, as a summary of our Catholic faith, says it thus: "By the power of the Holy Spirit he was born of the Virgin Mary, and became man." The Latin is even more expressive: "*ex* Maria Virgine," meaning not just *in* Mary but *of* Mary; of her being, of her flesh. On October 21, 1979, in a homily given in Pompeii, Pope John Paul put it this way: "In her human and virginal substance, she is overshadowed by the power of the Most High. Thanks to this power, and because of the Holy Spirit, she becomes Mother of the Son of God, though remaining a Virgin."[2]

Jesus was not only conceived but also *born* in a way that left his mother's virginity intact. The whole Church proclaims with Saint Augustine that "Mary 'remained a virgin in conceiving her Son, a virgin in giving birth to him, a virgin in carrying him, a virgin in nursing him at her breast, always a virgin.'"[3] Mary is definitely, in every sense of the term, "ever virgin."

But does not this affirmation clash with the dictates of reason? Undoubtedly it seems to. But the Gospel accounts (Mt 1:18–25 and Lk 1:26–38) present Mary's virginal conception as a work of God which goes not against but *beyond* all human understanding. "That which is conceived in her is of the Holy Spirit," the angel tells Joseph. The Church sees in this explanation the fulfillment of the prophet Isaiah's promise, "Behold, a virgin shall conceive and bear a son" (Is 7:14; cf. Mt 1:23). "And so the liturgy of the Church celebrates Mary as *Aeiparthenos,* the 'Ever-virgin'" (CCC 499).

There are those who try to interpret divine revelation in purely spiritual or otherwise partial terms. But direct and authoritative magisterial pronouncements such as this one make that escapism impossible.

How is a virginal birth possible? By the unlimited power of a most gracious God. We would do well to take to heart these words of Pope Saint Gregory I (FEF 3:2331): "We must understand that the divine operation, if comprehended by reason, is not remarkable; nor does that faith which human reason puts to the

test have merit. . . . The body of the Lord came into the presence
of the disciples through closed doors, which body, in truth, at His
birth came forth to human eyes from the closed womb of the Virgin. What wonder, then, if after His Resurrection and about to
reign victorious in eternity, He entered through closed doors,
who, coming so that He might die, came forth from the unopened
womb of the Virgin?"

The Old Testament

Ultimately, of course, the mystery is exactly that—a mystery of
faith, to be humbly received and reverenced. But a certain level of
understanding is possible. It is helpful to know, for instance, that
the key element of Isaiah 7:14, the Hebrew word *almah,* "was
translated by the Septuagint as *parthenos,* which usually but not in-
variably means virgin"; that "from the Septuagint, Matthew took
the quotation which he used in the infancy narrative"; and that
"*almah* is used nine times in the Old Testament, never for a married woman" (O'Carroll 1983, 130–131).[4] In that context it is
highly significant that the original text does not have a declarative,
sequential construction ("Behold, a virgin shall conceive and bear
a son"). It has a participial, simultaneous construction: "Behold a
virgin pregnant and *giving* birth."[5]

The Gospel of Matthew

We find in Matthew 1:18–25 the most important authentic interpretation of Isaiah 7:14. In the full sense of the prophecy, the "Emmanuel" is Jesus Christ—it is he who will save his people from
their sins—and the "virgin pregnant and giving birth" is holy
Mary.

Matthew directly affirms Mary's virginal conception of Jesus
not only in verses 22 and 23, where he declares Isaiah's prophecy
now fulfilled, but also in verses 18 and 20: "When his mother

Mary had been betrothed to Joseph, before they came together she was found to be with child of the Holy Spirit. . . . An angel of the Lord appeared to [Joseph] in a dream, saying, 'Joseph, son of David, do not fear to take Mary your wife, for that which is conceived in her is of the Holy Spirit. . . .'"

He also affirms it indirectly, in his presentation of Jesus' genealogy (1:1–17). It runs, "Abraham was the father of Isaac, and Isaac the father of Jacob, and Jacob the father of Judah and his brothers," and so on—until it gets to Jesus' immediate ancestry. There it suddenly changes direction: ". . . and Jacob the father of Joseph the husband of Mary, of whom Jesus was born, who is called Christ." Intention is revealed by context: Matthew excludes any involvement by Joseph in the conception of Jesus, but includes him in the fulfillment of the promise. The Messiah was to come from the house of David.[6] Legally, but not biologically, Joseph becomes the father of Jesus.

The Gospel of Luke

Luke first mentions Mary as "a virgin betrothed to a man whose name was Joseph, of the house of David" (1:27). The idea of a "virgin betrothed," strange as it sounds, makes good sense within the cultural context. At that time, as Father Ignace de la Potterie tells us (1992, 24), a Jewish marriage "took place in two stages. First, there was the making of a marriage contract. At this stage, the young couple did not live together. Both remained for a certain time within their respective families, and it was only after several weeks or several months (according to local custom) that they celebrated the second stage. Then the young bridegroom would solemnly go to search for his bride in the home of her parents, in order to introduce her to her own home. Only after this phase could they be seen together."

Luke presents us with a "virgin" who is "betrothed" but not yet living under the same roof as her husband. "Her legal marriage was already established. According to Jewish law, she was married to Joseph, but she did not yet live with him in his home" (de la Potterie 1992, 24). Thus, Mary's question "How can this be, since I have no husband?" both confirms her physical virginity and implies an intention to maintain it. The angel then confirms Mary in her virginity, which as a choice of lifestyle was in her day most unusual. In fact, "in the Jewish milieu to which Mary belonged, where the condition of remaining a virgin was considered a chastisement or even a malediction, a free choice of virginity was unthinkable" (de la Potterie 1992, 23). Nevertheless, the angel corroborates it. "The Holy Spirit will come upon you," he says, "and the power of the Most High will overshadow you . . ." (Lk 1:35).

Also highly significant is the parallel established between Mary's virginity and Elizabeth's sterility. The angel, by giving Mary the "sign" of Elizabeth as assurance that "nothing is impossible to God," implies that Mary's situation is as naturally and formidably an obstacle to pregnancy as is Elizabeth's advanced age. This would make no sense if "since I do not know man" simply meant "since I have not *as yet* made love to my husband."[7]

Finally, it should be noted that "for the 'fiat' of Mary at the Annunciation Luke employs the optative 'genoïto' without a subject which is used positively only in this unique place in the New Testament. In Greek, the optative expresses 'a *joyous desire* to,' never a resignation or a constraining submission before something burdensome and painful. The resonance of Mary's 'fiat' at the moment of the Annunciation is not that of the 'fiat voluntas tua' of Jesus in Gethsemane, nor that of a formula corresponding to the Our Father. Here there is a remarkable detail, which has only been noticed in recent years, and which even today is frequently lost from sight. The 'fiat' of Mary is not just a simple acceptance and even less, a resignation. It is rather a joyous desire to collaborate with what God foresees for her. It is the joy of total abandonment to the good will of God" (de la Potterie 1992, 35).

The Gospel of John

We can read of the virginal conception between the lines of Saint John's prologue on the Word of God: those who believe in the name of the Son of God, the eternal Word of the Father, "who were born not of blood nor of the will of the flesh nor of the will of man, but of God. And the Word became flesh and dwelt among us" (Jn 1:13–14).

An inconsistent objection

One objection to Mary's perpetual virginity which persists (particularly among those unfamiliar with the culture of biblical times) is based on the evangelists' allusions to the *brothers* of Jesus.[8] It's well known that in ancient Hebrew and Aramaic, which Jesus spoke, there were no specific words for degrees of relationship such as exist in most modern languages. In general, members of the same family, clan, or tribe were *brothers* including nephews, cousins, and other relatives. While, for example, we know from 2 Samuel 17:25 that Joab and Amasa were actually first cousins once removed, in 2 Samuel 20:9 Joab says to Amasa, "Is it well with you my brother?" The ambiguity is due to the deficient vocabulary of Hebrew and Aramaic in this particular case: they use the word *brother* for various kinds of relatives. Likewise, Matthew 13:55 refers to James and Joseph as Jesus' "brothers," but we know from Matthew 27:56 and John 19:25 that they were sons of Mary, the wife of Cleophas.

Teachings of the Fathers and of the magisterium

The Fathers of the Church agree in affirming Mary's perpetual virginity. Saints Athanasius, Gregory of Nyssa, Epiphanius of Salamis, Augustine of Hippo, Cyril of Alexandria—the list goes on and on.[9] As a matter of fact, says Father Juniper Carol (1956,

145), "even Harnack, a bitter foe of Mary's virginity, frankly admits that already in the second century this belief was unanimously accepted." From the fourth century on, the title "Ever Virgin" is used with great frequency and many works are dedicated to this subject.

A long series of Church pronouncements, from the Apostles' Creed to the Symbol of Constantinople (381) to the teaching of the Council of the Lateran (649), assure us of Mary's perpetual virginity. Canon 3 of the Lateran Council is particularly explicit: "If anyone does not, according to the holy Fathers, confess truly and properly that holy Mary, ever virgin and immaculate, is Mother of God, since in this latter age she conceived in true reality without human seed from the Holy Spirit, God the Word Himself, who before the ages was born of God the Father, and gave birth to Him without corruption, her virginity remaining equally inviolate after the birth, let him be condemned" (ND 703). The Second Vatican Council likewise declared that the "union of the Mother with the Son in the work of salvation is . . . manifest also at the birth of Our Lord, who did not diminish His mother's virginal integrity but sanctified it, when the Mother of God joyfully showed her firstborn Son to the shepherds and Magi" (LG 57).

Reason vis-à-vis the mystery

As we said earlier, the mystery of Mary's virginal motherhood eludes the grasp of reason. Nevertheless, it constitutes an intellectual scandal only for those who do not believe in the existence or omnipotence of God. Did God create the universe? Did God cause the "big bang"? Is God the Creator of all life? Did God infuse into matter the breath of life—what we call a soul—to give rise to the creature that we call the human being? If the answer to all these questions is yes, then how can it be impossible for this same God—this infinitely creative God—to "overshadow" Mary so that she can virginally conceive a son in and of her own flesh?

To consider this impossible is to side *against* intelligibility, not with it. It is to deny the creative power of God, and therefore God himself, and therefore the meaning of anything and everything, including human reason. No one who acknowledges God as the transcendent First Cause of everything that exists can reasonably deny God's ability to have a woman conceive without the involvement of a man.

God's reasons for wanting his mother to be a virgin

The *Catechism of the Catholic Church* summarizes, in nos. 503–507, the "mysterious reasons" that "the eyes of faith can discover in Revelation about why God in his saving plan wanted his son to be born of a virgin. These reasons touch both on the person of Christ and his redemptive mission, and on the welcome Mary gave that mission on behalf of all men" (CCC 502). Among the reasons cited are: "Mary's virginity manifests God's absolute initiative in the Incarnation. . . . The spousal character of the human vocation in relation to God (cf. 2 Cor 11:2) is fulfilled perfectly in Mary's virginal motherhood" (CCC 503, 505).

Third- and fourth-century authors considered the topic of Mary's virginal conception as a sign and manifestation of the divine Word: they concluded that God could be born only of a virgin and that only a virgin could conceive God. And, in the thirteenth century, Saint Thomas summarized the tradition: "Christ's human generation had to reflect his divine generation" (ST III, q. 28, 1.1–3).

Certainly we see how fitting it is that the only-begotten Son of the Father have a mother but no natural father, and that he not be conceived by the will of man (cf. Jn 1): for the purpose of his incarnation was to raise us to a new, supernatural, divine filiation.

The anthropological and eschatological
significance of her virginity

Mary's virginal motherhood is a reflection of the great value of virginity—both spiritual and bodily virginity in God's eyes. Virginity is even greater than the sacrament of marriage to which most of the faithful are called by a truly divine vocation, and which Mary herself, of course, shared. Far from leaving a person incomplete, a virginity like that of Mary—a virginity for undivided dedication to God—perfects and makes a person fruitful beyond all expectation.

John Paul II wrote: "In spite of having renounced physical fecundity, the celibate person becomes spiritually fruitful, the father and mother of many, cooperating in the realization of the family according to God's plan."[10] The perpetual virginity of Mary makes her a lofty symbol of the new order established by the Holy Spirit: the eschatological existence of the Kingdom of God: "For in the resurrection they neither marry nor are given in marriage, but are like angels in heaven" (Mt 22:30). Certainly our Lord said, "not all men can receive this precept, but only those to whom it is given. . . . He who is able to receive this, let him receive it" (Mt 19:11, 12).

1. Council of the Lateran: ND 703.
2. "The Son's Mission Begins with Mary's 'Fiat'": OR 12/3/79.
3. CCC 510; see also FEF 3:1289, 1518, 2177, 2194.
4. See also Carol 1956, 33–34.
5. See Scheeben 1:105–106.
6. See Is 16:5; Jer 23:5–6; Ez 37:24–28.
7. See de la Potterie 1992, 13, 33–34.
8. Cf. Mt 13:55; Mk 3:31-32; Jn 7:3-5; Ac 1:14.
9. See FEF 1:767a; 2:1020a, 1089a; 3:1518, 2133.
10. Pope John Paul II, *Familiaris Consortio* (November 22, 1981), 16.

4. *The Assumption of the Blessed Virgin Mary*

THE ASSOCIATION of Mary with the mystery of the Incarnate Word and Redeemer could not end on earth, but would reach its fullness in heaven, where the Blessed Mother unceasingly exercises, in union with her Son, his saving influence on the world. United to our Savior in the mystery of the Incarnation, united to him also in his work of redemption, she is, quite rightly, united with him as well in the triumph of his resurrection, in his exercise of dominion over all creation.

"Assumption"

In Mariology the term "assumption" has a meaning which is exclusively passive: a meaning applicable only to Mary (the one assumed), never to God (who did the assuming). It also has a meaning that is active with respect to Mary: she is assumed into heaven in virtue of the glorious union of her soul and body. However, the glorious vigor of Mary's soul is itself a gift, a grace, from God. Therefore, to avoid confusion, we prefer to affirm that Mary, body and soul, *was assumed* into heaven by the power of God, whereas Christ, the God-Man, *rose* to heaven by his own divine power.

We do, in a sense, also speak of the assumption of persons who die in the state of grace: "She has been taken to a better place"; "God bore him away"; "God took her to himself." Here, as in the case of Mary's Assumption, the term has a clearly passive meaning, but there is an important difference. Here we do not have in mind a psychosomatic event; we are not talking about an assumption of both soul and body. Only the souls of the just, not their bodies, have been taken to heaven; their bodies will have to wait for the general resurrection, which will take place at the end of time. In contrast, when we speak of the Assumption of the Blessed Virgin Mary, we are talking about a psychosomatic event: a simultaneous transfer of soul and body, of the entire person, to heaven.

Content of the dogma

On November 1, 1950, in the apostolic constitution *Munificentissimus Deus,* Pope Pius XII defined as a dogma of faith the Assumption of Mary. The decisive words are these: "We pronounce, declare, and define it to be a divinely revealed dogma: that the Immaculate Mother of God, the ever Virgin Mary, having completed the course of her earthly life, was assumed body and soul into heavenly glory" (section 44).

Mary's bodily glory was not, in other words, to be postponed until the end of time, as is the case with the rest of us. Nor did her body even begin to decompose. Mary was, in the words of Pope Paul VI, "likened to her risen Son in anticipation of the future lot of all the just."[1]

Mary's transition into heaven

In his dogmatic definition, Pope Pius XII deliberately left open the question of whether or not Mary died. "Having completed the course of her earthly life" accommodates either possibility. His definition neither affirms nor denies Mary's death and so the question remains open.

But clearly the Mother of God's most holy body didn't corrupt at all. If Mary's soul did separate from her body momentarily, the two were immediately reunited. We might consider her singular death as a sound sleep or ecstasy immediately preceding her Assumption. Undoubtedly, God's omnipotence and love for his mother do imply that he looked after every detail of her Assumption. Mystically speaking, Mary almost died on Calvary in her collaboration with the redemption of Christ. As Pope Leo XIII said in his encyclical *Iucunda Semper,* when she stood by the cross of Jesus, Mary "in her heart died with him, stabbed by the sword of sorrow" (PDM 93). We may assume, then, that her transition was altogether happy and exempt from suffering.[2]

Bases of the dogma

Pope Pius XII based his dogmatic definition on the following three grounds:

a) "The universal agreement of the Church's ordinary teaching authority" (MD 12; see also sections 36 and 41). In sections 14–17 the Holy Father discusses the "various testimonies, indications and signs of this common belief of the Church" (see section 13). "Sacred buildings are mentioned. The witness of the Liturgy is recalled with a reminder from the Pope that it does not 'engender the Catholic faith, but rather springs from it.' When he passes in review the opinions of the Fathers and Doctors, he states that 'they spoke of this doctrine as something already known and accepted by Christ's faithful'" (O'Carroll 1983, 56).

b) The fact that "the Sacred Writings . . . set the loving Mother of God as it were before our very eyes as most intimately joined to her divine Son and as always sharing his lot. . . . It seems impossible to think of her, the one who conceived Christ, brought him forth, nursed him with her milk, held him in her arms, and clasped him to her breast, as being apart from him in body, even though not in soul, after this earthly life" (MD 38).

c) The harmony of "the bodily Assumption of the loving Mother of God with her other prerogatives and privileges" (MD 21).

Mary's immediate glorification when the course of her earthly life was over seems to be demanded by her Son's love for his mother. From the moment our Redeemer became Mary's Son, as a perfect observer of divine law he couldn't help but honor his eternal Father and his beloved mother. Since he was able to give her eternal honor and glory and to preserve her from corruption, it's reasonable to conclude that he did so.

Mary's virginal motherhood, especially her virginity in giving birth, leads us to her incorruption when we consider Mary's most holy body. So gracious and divinely possessed a body couldn't be bound by corruption: we could affirm that it demanded the splendor of glory.

Moreover, "our own aspiration to eternal life takes on wings when we reflect on our heavenly Mother above who sees us and contemplates us tenderly."[3] Mary assumed into heaven is an image and foreshadowing of the pilgrim Church in heaven, and therefore she is the focus of hope and consolation for the pilgrim Church on earth.

Mary's Assumption reminds us of her power to intercede for us before God and she invites us to prayer of petition. Just as the risen Christ "lives to make intercession" (Heb 7:25), Mary, immediately glorified, lives to intercede for each one of her children. Popular piety and Marian art represent the mystery of the Assumption when the Blessed Virgin among clouds is borne away to heaven by angels. Although their intervention may be unnecessary, Saint Thomas sees in it a manifestation of the homage the angels and all creatures render to the glorified.[4]

1. Pope Paul VI, *The Credo of the People of God.*
2. See Scheeben 2:153.
3. Paul VI, *Allocution*, 15 August 1963; LG 68; Cf. Second Vatican Council, *Sacrosanctum Concilium*, 103.
4. See ST, q.84, a.1, ad 1.

5. Mary's Queenship

THE MYSTERY of the Assumption is accompanied by another Marian privilege very dear to the People of God: the crowning of Mary most holy as Queen of all creation. When she "was taken up body and soul into heavenly glory," proclaimed the Second Vatican Council, Mary was "exalted by the Lord as Queen of the universe, that she might be the more fully conformed to her Son, the Lord of lords [see Rev 19:16] and the conqueror of sin and death" (LG 59).

Pope John Paul II, in his encyclical *Redemptoris Mater*, says this: "The Mother of Christ is glorified as 'Queen of the Universe' (LG 59). She who at the Annunciation called herself the 'handmaid of the Lord' remained throughout her earthly life faithful to what this name expresses. In this she confirmed that she was a true 'disciple' of Christ, who strongly emphasized that his mission was one of service: the Son of Man 'came not to be served but to serve, and to give his life as a ransom for many' (Mt 20:28). In this way Mary became the first of those who 'serving Christ in others" with humility and patience lead their brothers and sisters to that King for whom to serve is to reign (LG 36), and she fully obtained that 'state of royal freedom' proper to Christ's disciples: to serve means to reign!" (RM 41).

Theological grounds for Mary's queenship

a) *Her divine motherhood*. As Pope Pius XII observes in his encyclical *Ad Caeli Reginam*, "the first to proclaim the royal office of Mary was the heavenly messenger, the archangel Gabriel" (AC: OL 702). "The Gospel, speaking of the Son to be conceived by the Virgin, says: 'He shall be called the Son of the Most High and the Lord God shall give unto Him the throne of David His Father, and He shall reign in the house of Jacob forever, and of His kingdom there shall be no end' (Lk 1:32–33), and, again, Mary is called 'Mother of the Lord' (Lk 1:43).

Hence it is easy to conclude that Mary is herself Queen, since she gave birth to a Son who, at the very moment of His conception, by reason of the hypostatic union of His human nature with the Word, was even as man King and Lord of all things" (AC: OL 701).

b) Her participation in the work of redemption. Quoting the anonymous author of *De mysteriis vitae Christi,* Pope Pius declares that "just as Christ, because He redeemed us, is by a special title our King and our Lord, so too is Blessed Mary [our Queen and our Mistress] because of the unique way in which she cooperated in our redemption. She provided her very substance for His body, she offered Him willingly for us, and she took a unique part in our salvation by desiring it, praying for it, and so obtaining it" (AC: OL 704).

From this he concludes the following: "Mary in the work of redemption was by God's will joined with Jesus Christ, the cause of salvation, in much the same way as Eve was joined with Adam, the cause of death. Hence it can be said that the work of our salvation was brought about by a 'restoration' [Saint Irenaeus] in which the human race, just as it was doomed to death by a virgin, was saved by a virgin" (AC: OL 705).

c) Her role in distributing the fruits of the Redemption. She is called *Omnipotentia Suplex,* the all-powerful supplicant. To this effect, Pope Leo XIII wrote: "the Most Blessed Virgin was granted almost unlimited power in dispensing graces" [AP: OL 169]. And Pope Saint Pius X adds that Mary carries out this office "as by a mother's right" (AD: OL 235*).*

A queen who rules

In sum, Mary is Queen because she is Mother of the King, and because she is so closely associated with Christ the Redeemer and

Sanctifier. She is no mere figurehead; she actually, with Christ, rules the created universe. She, with Christ, rules time and history.

To rule, properly speaking, involves taking initiative and making decisions. Let us not forget Mary's demonstrated capabilities in this area. In Cana, at a wedding feast where she is one of many guests (see Jn 2:1–11), we find her in the center of activity—in the area where food and wine are being served. When the wine runs out, Mary takes initiative: she decides it is time for Jesus to manifest his supernatural power, his identity as Messiah. And although according to Jesus that time has not yet come, he accepts Mary's suggestion. In just this way—this simple, feminine, effective way—the Mother of God rules as Queen the history of humanity. Very gently, with the utmost respect for the freedom of each one, she governs the lives of all her children.

Contemporary events like the private revelations at Fatima reflect the reality of Mary's direct intervention in history, of her actually changing the course of it. The benevolent intervention of Mary is not, however, limited to momentous historical events. Everyone who sets out on the interior journey of a Christian life will have personal experiences to relate—very clear, if not empirically demonstrable—of the intervention of the Blessed Virgin in the transcendent moments of their lives. In fact, our mother in heaven takes a very active interest in every moment of our lives.

To reign is to serve

In section 10 of the *Letter of Pope John Paul II to Women* we find a beautiful commentary on the mystery of Mary's queenship:

> *The Church sees in Mary the highest expression of the "feminine genius" and she finds in her a source of constant inspiration. Mary called herself the "handmaid of the Lord" (Lk 1:38). Through obedience to the Word of God she accepted her lofty yet not easy vocation as wife and mother in the*

family of Nazareth. Putting herself at God's service, she also put herself at the service of others: a *service of love.* Precisely through this service Mary was able to experience in her life a mysterious, but authentic "reign." It is not by chance that she is invoked as "Queen of heaven and earth." The entire community of believers thus invokes her; many nations and peoples call upon her as their "Queen." *For her, "to reign" is to serve! Her service is "to reign"!*

This is the way in which authority needs to be understood, both in the family and in society and the Church. Each person's fundamental vocation is revealed in this "reigning," for each person has been created in the "image" of the One who is Lord of heaven and earth and called to be his adopted son or daughter in Christ. Man is the only creature on earth "which God willed for its own sake," as the Second Vatican Council teaches; it significantly adds that man "cannot fully find himself except through a sincere gift of self" (GS 24).

The maternal "reign" of Mary consists in this. She who was, in all her being, a gift for her Son *has also become a gift for the sons and daughters of the whole human race,* awakening profound trust in those who seek her guidance along the difficult paths of life on the way to their definitive and transcendent destiny. Each one reaches this *final goal* by fidelity to his or her own vocation; this goal provides meaning and direction for the earthly labors of men and women alike.

6. Mary's Cooperation in our Sanctification

WE TURN our attention now to a fact which affects us profoundly. The whole magnificent array of marvels with which God
has graced Mary—her Immaculate Conception, her perpetual virginity, her divine motherhood, her Assumption into heaven, her
queenship—has not been given to her solely for her own sake or
even for that of her Son. These gifts are intended to benefit all of
us as well. Just as the Word became flesh "for us men and for our
salvation," so, too, was Mary conceived in the mind of God, and
consequently in her mother's womb. She was created to help
restore and bring to fruition the original plan of God for the
human race by cooperating in its redemption and in its elevation
into the life of the Trinity.

In this chapter we will study more directly Mary's role in the
work of redemption and sanctification. So relevant is she that
Pope John Paul II speaks of her actual "cooperation" and "collaboration": her "cooperation with the Savior's whole mission
through her actions and sufferings"; her "collaboration with the
work of her Son, the Redeemer" (RM 39).

Since, in the economy of salvation, redemption implies sanctification, a collaboration in the one work implies a collaboration
in the other as well. So if the "participation" of Mary "in God's
plan for man's salvation through the mystery of the Redemption
is . . . unique in profundity and range of action" (RH 22), it must
somehow also be a vital element in our sanctification. But is Mary,
properly speaking, a *cause* of our redemption and sanctification in
the Mystical Body of Christ?

God did in fact, in his free and eternal design, choose to associate with the work of his Son one woman, Mary, to such an
extent that she too would truly be the cause of the salvation of the
human race. This may sound like hyperbole, but it is the literal

truth. And it fits in perfectly with all the other mysteries involved in the Redemption and taught by the Church.

To grasp this truth, let us first consider the general outline of God's plans for mankind both before and after the Fall.

Original sin and the unity of the human race

We often ask ourselves, How is it possible that the sin of Adam and Eve is transmitted by generation to all their descendants, no matter how far removed they are, in time, from that lamentable fall? Why should I have to suffer for a sin committed by people who lived eons ago? What do they have to do with me?

Posed in such a way, the question is difficult if not impossible to answer. We need not question the fact of an inherited tragedy, an inherited inclination toward sin. The fact is plain to see; we live with it every day. And it would certainly not behoove us children of God to even try to call to account that Father who sacrificed the life of his only-begotten Son for the sake of our eternal salvation. What we need to do is to delve into the mystery of original sin and its obvious consequences and see if we can find for ourselves a satisfactory answer, no matter how mysterious, and thereby be confirmed in the truth. We must not fear true mystery, for it is always a light that reveals to us more than we could have hoped for.

If I find in my blood and in my spirit the toxic fallout of original sin, there has got to be a good reason for it, and that reason must somehow be grounded in the absolute, universal principle of the love of God. There, in a nutshell, is our answer.

God created us human beings in his own image and likeness. God, one in nature, is three Persons. He is triune: one in three, three in one; unity in plurality, diversity in unity. In a homily given to the people of Puebla de Los Angeles on January 28, 1979, Pope John Paul made this beautiful statement: "God in His deepest mystery is not a solitude, but a family, since He has in Himself fatherhood, sonship, and the essence of the family, which is love."[1] God created us male and female so that together we could form one family, a "one" in the image of the God-Family. The number and variety of members of the great human family is no obstacle to its unity, just as diversity of Persons is no obstacle to the unity of the one true God.

There is, of course, the basic difference that the three divine Persons are one and the same being—together they have but one, undivided nature—whereas each human person is a separate being, with a numerically distinct nature. Nevertheless, the nature of all human beings is essentially the same. While it is true that every human person is a new and distinct creation, it is also true that human nature is multiplied by generation. Procreation gives rise to unique persons who share the same nature. As different as we may be, we all have the same basic nature as that of Adam and Eve, who were created to be "two in one flesh," a unity in their plurality, with a common essence and purpose. Together they were commissioned to "be fruitful and multiply," to be the parents of a large, close-knit family that would fill first the earth and afterwards heaven. Made in the image and likeness of God, they were to originate a family that would reflect the unity of the divine Family, wherein each Person exists entirely in the others.

According to God's original plan, the members of the human family were to enjoy not only a biological, affective, and spiritual unity among themselves, but also a shared participation in the supernatural life of sanctifying grace (see ND 1984/23). There was to be among them a communion—a common union—both in human life as such and in the life of the three divine Persons. This plan announced by God, this plan that only God could make possible, was for the human family to have, in and through its diversity, a real unity.

Sin, to a terrible extent, sabotaged this plan. Adam and Eve fractured within themselves the bond with God which was the bond of their unity. And so, since they could not give what they did not have, human life was transmitted without its original preternatural and supernatural gifts. Instead, it would be fraught with divisions caused by sin: divisions separating people from God and from one another. The human family lost much of its cohesiveness, and the result was murder (see Gn 4:1–8). Human nature was multiplied without the supernatural life of grace God had given it at its inception, and with, instead, the weakness of a creation seriously alienated from its Creator.

Nevertheless, the human family would still have a basic solidarity. In theological parlance, this term means much more than a mere sentiment, desire, inclination, or activity. It means that common union, that vital communion, that stream of life—mysterious, imperceptible to the senses, but very real—that has always run through our great human family. The fate of one member is vitally linked with that of every other member.[2] Unfortunately, sin made us all share the experience of evil. We are born into a "common union" marked by the evil caused by our first parents. But "O happy fault!" sings the Church, in her Easter Proclamation. "O happy fault, . . . which gained for us so great a Redeemer!" Bad and undesirable as it is in itself, what good fortune our involvement in original sin has proved to be, since it occasioned God's showing us how incredibly much he loves us. What original sin ended up "meriting" for us—such is the greatness of God's love—was a Redeemer who is God himself, the second divine Person, the Word made flesh in the immaculate womb of the Blessed Virgin Mary.

Yet our Triune God continues to long for what Christ Jesus, just before consummating our redemption, asked from the Father: "that they may all be one; even as thou, Father, art in me, and I in thee, that they also may be in us . . ." (Jn 17:21). "By his Incarnation," said the Second Vatican Council, "he, the Son of God, in a certain way united himself with each man."[3] Commenting on this text, Pope John Paul writes (in RH 13):

What is in question here is man in all his truth, in his full magnitude. We are not dealing with the "abstract" man, but the real, "concrete," "historical" man. We are dealing with "each" man, for each one is included in the mystery of the Redemption and with each one Christ has united Himself for ever through this mystery. Every man comes into the world through being conceived in his mother's womb and being born of his mother, and precisely on account of the mystery of the Redemption is entrusted to the solicitude of the Church. Her solicitude is about the whole man and is focused on him in an altogether special manner. The object of her care is man in his unique unrepeatable human reality, which keeps intact the image and likeness of God Himself (cf. Gn 1:26). The Council points out this very fact when, speaking of that likeness, it recalls that "man is the only creature on earth that God willed for itself" (GS 24). Man as "willed" by God, as "chosen" by Him from eternity and called, destined for grace and glory—this is "each" man, "the most concrete" man, "the most real"; this is man in all the fullness of the mystery in which he has become a sharer in Jesus Christ, the mystery in which each one of the four thousand million human beings living on our planet has become a sharer from the moment he is conceived beneath the heart of his mother.

These words from Pope John Paul shine with a light that permits us to see as clearly as possible the marvelous mystery of the Mystical Body of Christ, and, within that specific context, our union with Christ and Mary. The Mystical Body of Christ is in reality a purification and an elevation of the mystical body which mankind has been from the very beginning.

There is a moment in Christ's life when he reveals God's purpose in creating and redeeming us. That is the moment in which he says, "that they may all be one"—not "one" in just any way, but "as thou, Father, art in me, and I in thee." "Holy Father," he prays,

"keep them in thy name, which thou hast given me, that they may
be one, even as we are one. . . . The glory which thou hast given
me I have given to them, that they may be one even as we are one,
I in them and thou in me, that they may become perfectly one, so
that the world may know that thou hast sent me and hast loved
them even as thou hast loved me" (Jn 17:11, 22–23).

These are words of incomparable greatness and depth. God
wants each and all of us to be immersed in his own life, in the intimate life of the Trinity, so thoroughly that one day the divine Word
will be able to say, as we might phrase it, "Just as you, Father, are
in me and I am in you, they too are so truly one that they are one
single entity, one single nature."

How is such an astounding mystery at all possible? It is sin that
has confused our understanding. Actually, all of humanity has from
the very beginning been, in a real sense, one. We all have the same
first parents; we form with them a real unit, inasmuch as our very
being derives from theirs. That is why their sin, though personally
theirs alone, is ours by nature. It was not "original" in only a
chronological sense; it was also originating. Like a chromosomal
defect, it runs in the family—the entire family of mankind. "The
whole human race," explains the *Catechism*, "is in Adam 'as one
body of one man' (Saint Thomas Aquinas, *De Malo* 4, 1). . . . Adam
had received original holiness and justice not for himself alone, but
for all human nature. By yielding to the tempter, Adam and Eve
committed a *personal sin,* but this affected the *human nature* that
they would then transmit *in a fallen state.* It is a sin which will be
transmitted by propagation to all mankind, that is, by the transmission of a human nature deprived of original holiness and justice. And that is why original sin is called 'sin' only in an analogi-
cal sense: it is a sin 'contracted' and not 'committed'—a state and
not an act" (CCC 404).

The key, then, to understanding original sin is to focus less on
guilt and more on relationship. The question to ask is not, Why
do I have to take the blame for someone else's sin? but rather, Why

is it that I am so inclined toward sin? And the answer is this: It is because I am one with those first parents of mine. Being "two in one flesh," they could not pass down to me anything better than what they had made of themselves. There is a vital, inescapable solidarity among those who have the same blood running in their veins. And since, in the case of us human beings, our entire body—blood and bones and everything else—is personal (belonging to a person, a being with a spiritual soul), there is a spiritual as well as physical solidarity among all members of the human race. In a mysterious but literally natural way, we are one with our first parents, who were one with each other.

Sin wounded the original unity of the human race; it sabotaged God's plan. But God is not disposed toward losing the family that he has created in his own image and likeness. He sends his only-begotten Son into the world to become one of us; and the infinitely unitive force of Christ's love not only restores and intensifies our lost unity, but even raises it into the unity of the Triune God. It is a marvel as certain as it is amazing. So certain that Saint Augustine, that powerful intellect fueled by faith, dares to make this bold synthesis: "In what concerns these two men [Adam and Christ], . . . the Christian faith properly consists."[4] Thanks to that solidarity, a marvelous interchange takes place between Christ and sinful mankind: Christ takes upon himself all our sins and makes infinite satisfaction for them before the Father. We can now be interiorly renewed by the grace of God. We can be "made righteous" by having the merits of Christ's life, passion, and death applied to ourselves (see Rom 5:19). It is true that because of our natural solidarity with Adam, "death reigned . . . even over those whose sins were not like the transgression of Adam" (Rom 5:14). But we have a more powerful natural solidarity with Christ, who, as the new and permanent Head of the human race, restored, revitalized, and upgraded its capacity for holiness and divine filiation. "The redemptive act," said Pope John Paul II in his general audience of August 31, 1983, "has inserted the human person into Christ, making him a sharer in the divine sonship of the Word: we are sons in the Only Begotten Son of the Father."[5]

Only in this light is it possible to understand original sin and the redemption accomplished by Christ. And only from within that context can we appreciate the mystery of Mary, the new Eve.

Mary, the new Eve, mother of the living

Adam did nothing of significance without Eve, and vice versa. Actually, no person—human or divine—does anything all alone (see ND 315). But here our focus is on the beginnings of human life. The human family has a father and a mother; both are essential to that unity whereby we are made in the image and likeness of the Triune God.

It is true that the work of restoring our lost unity and elevating it into the intimate life of the Trinity could have been accomplished by the Incarnate Word without the involvement of any other human person. Being both divine and human, he himself was (and is) the only strictly necessary bridge between heaven and earth. Symmetry on a human level was not an absolute requirement.

However, neither should it be regarded as a superfluous luxury—or, still worse, as a condition incompatible with Jesus Christ's identity as our one and only Savior. As Saint Augustine says, "Christ Jesus is Mediator of God and of men, not in that He is God but in that He is Man" (FEF 3:1836). Without some kind of symmetry on a human level, our redemption would have been less human, less in accord with human nature, than in fact it was. Had our Redeemer acted as a solitary individual, his identity as the new Adam (see 1 Cor 15:22, 45) would have been less obvious. Jesus Christ is God made thoroughly human in order to bring human oneness to its ultimate, blessed destiny.

Although God could have redeemed by himself, he did not want to. It was not fitting for the Redeemer to redeem alone; for the Sanctifier to sanctify alone; for the Word to divinize alone. Luther's fear that cooperative action on the part of a creature obscures, diminishes, or even annuls the action of God is entirely unfounded. It was the decision of God himself, the decision of the Blessed Trinity, to carry out not only the work of creation but also the work of redemption in this way: with the cooperation of human beings. Witness Saint Paul: "Now I rejoice in my sufferings for your sake, and in my flesh I complete what is lacking in Christ's afflictions for the sake of his body, that is, the Church . . ." (Col 1:24). Christ counts on Paul for the life of the Church and for the salvation of the world. Paul, simply as a faithful Christian, is in on Christ's work of salvation. Without Christ, Paul would be nothing. But being with Christ—being, in fact, incorporated into Christ's Mystical Body (see 1 Cor 12:12–27)—Paul is one with the Redeemer. Paul does not multiply or divide the Redeemer; rather, by God's loving design, he is included in the activity of the one Redeemer. Far from casting a shadow on Christ's work, or from annulling it altogether, Paul manifests it as something unspeakably magnanimous, full of generous mercy. He—and each of us as well—is invited and expected to cooperate, to collaborate, with our Redeemer in the work of redemption. God chose to unite us sinners to himself even in the work of redemption; in the very process of his freeing us from our sins and opening to us the gates of heaven.

Well, if Paul and every one of us are called to be one with Christ, with a unity like that of our Triune God, what must have been the unity formed between Christ and his mother? How tightly bonded they must be! Mary's unity with Christ must be qualitatively superior to that of any other creature.

Mary's role in the work of her Son is not just to keep him company. Nor is it only to intercede with him on our behalf. Although many do emphasize this activity above all others, and although Mary is a most powerful supplicant, her role is not limited to intercession. Mary, declared the Second Vatican Council, "is joined by an inseparable bond to the saving work of her Son" (SC 103). In the entire length and breadth of the saving work of Christ (without which she, too, would be nothing), Mary is involved in a most intimate way, even more so than Eve was in the original sin that made it necessary. If Eve was fully immersed in that first sin, Mary has been fully immersed in Christ from the first instant of her life.

When God said prophetically to the serpent (Satan), "I will put enmity between you and the woman" (see Gn 3:15), he inseparably linked a woman (Mary) with Satan's future conqueror (Christ). From all eternity God thought of Mary as being one with Christ, the Head of redeemed humanity, and as sharing in that same destiny of saving the fallen world. God's wisdom, always at work in our individual and collective histories despite Satan's efforts to thwart it, is manifest in this great design. For "since the invincible enmity against the serpent is represented as common to both [the woman and her seed], the victory must also be common to both in one way or another; and this is shown by the text which has the obvious purpose of making the punishment of the serpent complete, since a woman is the instrument of his defeat, as the first woman is the instrument of his victory" (Scheeben 1:242).

Mary's union with Christ is full and explicit from the moment of her *fiat*. Understood in all its breadth, her divine motherhood radically justifies and even necessitates Mary's intimate, intense, and all-encompassing participation in the life and mission of the Incarnate Word. In fact, her participation extends throughout the history of redemption and sanctification. As Pope John Paul says, Mary "constantly 'precedes' the Church in her journey through human history" (RM 49). "It is precisely in this ecclesial journey or pilgrimage through space and time, and even more through the history of souls, that Mary is present, as the one who is 'blessed because she believed,' as the one who advanced on the pilgrimage of faith, sharing unlike any other creature in the mystery of Christ" (RM 25).

In Mary's womb the Word became flesh. That key event of history, which reaches from Adam to the last human being on earth, is utterly unique. For "if Mary is really the one giving birth to God, if she bears him who is the death of death and is life in the full sense of the word, this being the Mother of God is really a 'new birth' (*nova nativitas*): a new way of giving birth inserted into the old way . . ." (Ratzinger 1983, 77–78). Mary is one with Christ in every moment and every phase of his redemptive life and death. If Eve is present, in a certain active sense, in the flesh and blood of every last mortal, Mary is—from the moment of her *fiat*—much more actively present in the lives of all the living.

God himself arranged things this way. And it involves no question whatsoever of putting Mary before Christ. The mystery must, in fact, be contemplated precisely from the opposite perspective. The centrality of Christ is the supreme reason for Mary's involvement in all our relations with him. If Christ is Head of the Church, that reality of itself implies Mary's identity as Mother of the Church. "Mary's 'motherhood' of the Church is the reflection and extension of her motherhood of the Son of God" (RM 24).

God's purpose in sending us Christ, says Saint Paul, was "to unite all things in him, things in heaven and things on earth" (Eph 1:9–10). Saint Irenaeus, commenting on this text, interprets it thus: "The Word, becoming man, recapitulates all things in Himself, so that . . . He might at the proper time draw all things to Himself."[6] The Son of God "became what we are, *so that* He might bring us to be what He Himself is."[7] All that Adam, the first head of the human family, had lost for it by sinning, Christ came to restore: goodness, truth, beauty; harmony, order, solidarity. The universe was without a head; or, perhaps even worse, it had a head deranged by sin, a head incapable of steering it in the direction of the Triune God. The original order, truth, goodness, beauty of creation had to be reinstated and brought to fruition. When the Word became flesh, humanity and the entire universe had for the first time a really viable, reliable head. Jesus Christ, perfect God and perfect man, with us for good, reveals to us the mysteries of our own origin in the Father's love and our own destiny to live forever in the love of the Triune God. Quite literally he becomes for us "the way, and the truth, and the life" (Jn 14:6). Christ is indisputably the one and only Head of the Church. There is, as Saint Paul says, "one mediator between God and men, the man Christ Jesus . . ." (1 Tm 2:5). However, that one mediator chose to have one person, his own mother, uniquely united to him in his work of redemption and sanctification. Mary is, as we shall see, not just one of the redeemed, or one more member of Christ's Mystical Body. Not only excellent, she is eminent; more perfect, more grace-filled, than all the other members of that Body. She is most definitely in the Church, but somehow also above it. She is, indeed, "present in the mystery of the Church as a model. But the Church's mystery also consists in generating people to a new and immortal life: this is her motherhood in the Holy Spirit. And here Mary is not only the model and figure of the Church; she is much more. For, 'with maternal love she cooperates in the birth and development' of the sons and daughters of Mother Church" (RM 44).

If Adam was the head of the human family, right beside him was Eve; he did nothing without her. If Christ, the Word made flesh, is the new Adam, we can expect to find with him a new Eve (see Rom 5:12–21 and 1 Cor 15:22, 45). The Fathers of the Church readily found her in Christ's mother, the Blessed Virgin Mary.

In fact, from the middle of the second century, beginning with Saint Justin Martyr, Saint Irenaeus, and Tertullian (see FEF 1:141, 224, 358), the Fathers have expressly presented Mary as the new Eve. If Eve was in some way the beginning of every evil on earth, Mary was, said Saint Irenaeus, "'the beginning of all good things'" (see DT: OL 210). These testimonies multiply during the third and fourth centuries with Saint Epiphanius, Saint Ephraim of Syria, and the Cappadocian Fathers.[8] In the fifth century Saint

Augustine, Saint Cyril of Alexandria, and the Council of Ephesus laid the groundwork for development of the doctrine of Mary's spiritual motherhood.[9] In our own day the magisterium explicitly reiterates the teachings of the Church Fathers. Mary is truly "'the Mother of the living'"; we do indeed have "'death through Eve, life through Mary.'"[10] It was "by her obedience" that "she became the new Eve, mother of the living" (CCC 511). "The Blessed Virgin was on the earth the virgin Mother of the Redeemer, and above all others and in a singular way the generous associate and humble handmaid of the Lord. She conceived, brought forth, and nourished Christ, she presented Him to the Father in the temple, and was united with Him by compassion as He died on the cross. In this singular way she cooperated by her obedience, faith, hope and burning charity in the work of the Savior in giving back supernatural life to souls. Wherefore she is our mother in the order of grace" (LG 61).

Chapter 12 of the Book of Revelation bears striking witness to this mystery. The "woman clothed with the sun" has characteristics clearly identifying her as simultaneously the Blessed Virgin Mary and the Church. This woman "brought forth a male child, one who is to rule all the nations with a rod of iron, but her child was caught up to God and to his throne" (verse 5); clearly she is Mary, the mother of Jesus. But later "the dragon was angry with the woman, and went off to make war on the rest of her offspring, on those who keep the commandments of God and bear testimony to Jesus" (verse 17). Evidently, as Father Lucien Deiss says (1972, 139), the woman's child "is at the same time both the individual Messias and the entire assembly of the redeemed; he is Christ considered as containing within himself all those who belong to him. Hence the Mother of the Child is at the same time both Mary and the Church, Mary considered as the archetype of the Church." Father Deiss also charts impressive points of contact between Genesis 3 and Revelation 12 to demonstrate that "in her struggle against the Dragon, the ancient Serpent, the victorious

Woman clothed with the sun and crowned with stars takes the place of the first Eve; in Mary, God is mindful of Eve" (1972, 139–40).

The absolute source of all life, natural as well as supernatural, is, of course, the Blessed Trinity. But the Triune God grants creatures, in different ways and degrees, the capacity to give as well as receive life. In the case of human beings, this applies not only to natural life, but also to supernatural life. Our participation in divine life comes to us in the first place from the divine and human Christ—the new Adam, the new Head, the source of a new creation, of a new life—and in the second place, in and through and with him, from the creature most closely united with him: the Blessed Virgin Mary. Whereas Eve was the wife of the first Adam, Mary is one with Christ fundamentally as his mother. "By virtue of divine election Mary is the earthly mother of the Father's consubstantial Son and his 'generous companion' in the work of redemption" (RM 38; see also LG 61). Accommodating himself to what was most suitable for the human race as a whole, Christ deliberately associated with himself a woman in his work of redemption, to such an extent that through him and with him she would come to occupy an intimate and transcendent place in the history of every man and woman's salvation.

In sum, if Eve is the mother of the living unto death, Mary is even more profoundly the mother of the living unto eternal life.

It is proper for a mother to conceive, give life, procreate. Were Mary not to do this, she would not be a true mother. But she is our mother: she engenders in us the life of grace so that we live in Christ and, through him, in the Triune God.

Mary's spiritual motherhood

Obviously Mary is not our mother in a natural sense. Nevertheless, she is literally our mother. The "universal motherhood of

Mary, which is usually called the mystical motherhood, may not at all be considered a purely moral or so-called motherhood. In its nature it is as equally real, organic, living, and substantial a relation as that of the bodily motherhood. It rests on the maternal relation of Mary to Christ and the organic relation in which Christians stand to Christ as their Head" (Scheeben 1:232). In his encyclical *Ad Diem Illum* (see OL 229–30), Pope Saint Pius X expressed this truth most beautifully:

> Is not Mary the Mother of Christ? Then she is our Mother also. And we must in truth hold that Christ, the Word made flesh, is also the Savior of mankind. Now, as the God-Man, He had a material body like that of any other man; and as Savior of the human family, He had a spiritual and mystical body, the society, namely, of those who believe in Christ. "So we, being many, are one body in Christ" (Rom 12:5).
>
> Now the Blessed Virgin did not conceive the Eternal Son of God merely in order that He might be made man, taking His human nature from her, but also in order that by means of the nature assumed from her, He might be the Redeemer of men. For which reason the Angel said to the shepherds: "For this day is born to you a Savior who is Christ the Lord" (Lk 2:11).
>
> Therefore, in the same holy bosom of His most chaste Mother, Christ took to Himself flesh, and united to Himself the spiritual body formed by those who were to believe in Him. Hence Mary, carrying the Savior within her, may be said to have also carried all those whose life was contained in the life of the Savior. Therefore all who are united to Christ, and as the Apostle says, "are members of His body, of His flesh and of His bones" (Eph 5:30), have issued from the womb of Mary like a body united to His head. Hence, in a spiritual and mystical fashion, we are all children of Mary, and she is Mother of us all: as St. Augustine said, "the Mother spiritually, indeed, but truly the Mother of the members of Christ who we are."

Ours is an ineffable dignity, steeped in infinite mercy and goodness. Not only has the Spirit of the Father and the Son conformed us to the Son so that we too can exclaim "Abba! Father!" (Rom 8:15–16), but we are also given a filial relationship to Mary so that with her Son we too can exclaim "Mama! Mother!" Far from negating the consistency, the intensity, or the reality of Christian life, this relationship only confirms it.

The universality of Mary's motherhood

Because all human beings are in some way united to Christ by the very fact of the Incarnation, Mary's spiritual motherhood has a universal dimension. But is she a mother to every person, from the most holy to the most sinful, in the same way and degree? This question is answered indirectly by Saint Thomas Aquinas, in the distinctions he makes regarding Christ's headship. "Christ is," he says, "the Head of all men, but diversely. For, first and principally, He is the Head of such as are united to Him by glory; secondly, of those who are actually united to Him by charity; thirdly, of those who are actually united to Him by faith; fourthly, of those who are united to Him merely in potentiality, which is not yet reduced to act, yet will be reduced to act according to divine predestination; fifthly, of those who are united to Him in potentiality, which will never be reduced to act; such are those men existing in the world who . . . , on their departure from this world, wholly cease to be members of Christ, as being no longer in potentiality to be united to Christ" (ST III.8.3).

Accordingly, we can say that Mary is the Mother of the blessed in heaven in a sublime way; of persons on earth in the state of grace, in a perfect way (since they have a complete supernatural life); of Christians in the state of mortal sin, in an imperfect way (since they have only the first element of supernatural life, which is faith); of the nonbaptized, in a potential or de jure way (since Mary is destined by God to "birth" them into a perfect supernatural life); and of the condemned in hell, in no way (since they are no longer capable of union with Christ).

In any case, as long as we are still on this earth we can always cry out with Blessed Josemaría Escrivá: "My Mother! Mothers on earth look with greater love upon the weakest of their children, the one with the worst health, or who is least intelligent, or is a poor cripple.

"Sweet Lady, I know that you are more of a Mother than all other mothers put together. And, since I am your son, since I am weak, and ill, and crippled, and ugly . . ."[11]

Cooperating in the work of redemption

Realizing that Mary has, in Christ, been constituted as mother of God's children, let us now see how she merited, to some extent, that grace by which she became the new Eve, Christ's "generous companion in the work of redemption" (RM 38).

Mary's full mystical union with her son, the Son of God, is the fruit of the work of the Holy Spirit and of her responsiveness to that work. On that basis we can properly say that the Virgin of Nazareth has a "participation" in the "mystery of the Redemption" which is "unique in profundity and range of action" (RH 22). This participation begins at the Annunciation, when, as a representative of the entire human race, she gives her consent to a marriage between the Son of God and the human race (see RM 13 and ND 710). In freely consenting to become the Mother of God, she accepts within her very being the Incarnation of the Word, and is thereby inseparably connected to his work of redemption—in a subordinate, dependent, yet singular capacity. Her cooperation begins at the very moment of her *fiat,* when, never having been held back by the least attraction to sin, she commits her whole self—literally, explicitly, unreservedly—to the salvific will of God. Having just been called "Full of Grace" by an angel, and knowing that she is to be the Mother of God, she consecrates herself as "the handmaid of the Lord" to the person and the work of her Son (see RM 39).

Mary's identification with her Son—of this there can be no doubt—encompassed in principle God's entire plan of salvation. We are not at all surprised to find her "standing by the cross of Jesus"; she has, after all, long since known and accepted that one day "a sword will pierce through your own soul also" (Jn 19:25; Lk 2:35). As a matter of fact, the wording of that prophecy bears striking witness to the reality of Mary's union and participation with her Son in the work of redemption. "Behold," Simeon had said, "this child is set for the fall and rising of many in Israel, and for a sign that is spoken against (and a sword will pierce through your own soul also), that thoughts out of many hearts may be revealed." The Blessed Virgin, as the Second Vatican Council expressed it, "faithfully persevered in her union with her Son unto the cross, where she stood, in keeping with the divine plan, grieving exceedingly with her only begotten Son, uniting herself with a maternal heart with His sacrifice, and lovingly consenting to the immolation of this Victim which she herself had brought forth" (LG 58).

Arnold of Bonneval gave this truth a more vivid expression: "Doubtless there was one will between Christ and Mary, and both at the same time offered to God one sacrifice, the one in the blood of her heart, the other in the blood of His body" (see Scheeben 2:218). In the words of Pope Leo XIII, she "in her heart died with Him, stabbed by the sword of sorrow" (IS: PDM 93).

Mary suffered with Christ, in full mystical identification with him. As Blessed Josemaría says, "What could she do? She united herself fully with the redemptive love of her Son, and offered to the Father her immense sorrow, which pierced her pure heart like a sharp-edged sword" (*Friends of God,* 288).

Why did she accept without protest this torture? "In a miracle of love," says Pope Leo XIII, "so that she might receive us as her sons, [Mary] offered generously to Divine Justice her own Son" (IS: PDM 93). In union with her dying Son, Mary willingly suffered for us. Joyously and painlessly she had given birth to God. Now, however, she suffered grievously, to give us birth; to collaborate with her Son in making us, by God's design, both God's children and hers. Contemplation of this truth is enough to move even the hardest of hearts.

The Blessed Virgin unites her compassion to Christ's passion, her motherly tears to her Son's blood. She, with him, sacrifices; and thus she becomes our mother. " 'Standing by the cross of Jesus,'" says Pope John Paul, "Mary shares in the gift which the Son makes of himself: she offers Jesus, gives him over, and begets him to the end for our sake" (EV 103). She, with him, also merits. Certainly, as Pope Saint Pius X said, "grace comes from God alone. But since she surpassed all in holiness and union with Christ, and has been associated with Christ in the work of redemption, she, as the expression is, merits *de congruo* [by association] what Christ merits *de condigno* [by his own right], and is the principal minister in the distribution of grace" (AD: OL 234). "By the will of God," as Pope Pius XII expressed it, "the most Blessed Virgin Mary was inseparably joined with Christ in accomplishing the work of man's redemption, so that our salvation flows from the love of Jesus Christ and His sufferings intimately united with the love and sorrows of His Mother" (HA: OL 778).

Mother of the redeemed

More than Saint Paul or anyone else—indeed, in a qualitatively superior way—Mary "completes" in her body and especially in her soul that which, by Divine Providence, "is lacking in Christ's afflictions."[12] The redemptive value of her contribution is enormous, since she is not just one more person; she is the Mother of the Son of God. By cooperation with her own Redeemer, she is the spiritual Mother of all the redeemed (see LG 53). The reason is not so much that Jesus, from the cross, *proclaims* this reality (which he does). It is more that by this proclamation he basically "*highlights* a new relationship between Mother and Son, the whole truth and reality of which he solemnly *confirms*" (RM 23; emphasis added). In other words, he proclaims a reality which has already taken effect. Mary has been constituted Mother of the redeemed, Mother of the Church, by her full association with the sacrifice of her Son.

Mother of the Church and of divine grace

There is, then, a mysterious reality in Mary on account of which we can and should call her our mother. To quote, once more, the Second Vatican Council: "She is 'the mother of the members of Christ . . . having cooperated by charity that faithful might be born in the Church, who are members of that Head' (Saint Augustine, *De Sancta Virginitate*, 6). Wherefore she is hailed as a preeminent and singular member of the Church, and as its type and excellent exemplar in faith and charity. The Catholic Church, taught by the Holy Spirit, honors her with filial affection and piety as a most beloved mother" (LG 53).

Mary's identity as Mother of the Church does not, then, place her outside the Church. On the contrary, she is "a preeminent and singular member of the Church." As Mother of God, she is adorned with all those special graces that God lavished on her so that she could be the worthy mother of his Son.[13] Intimately united to God, and to the redemptive work of Christ, "by her obedience, faith, hope and burning charity" (see LG 61), she is the "type and excellent exemplar" of the Church and its saving action. Absolutely all the grace that comes to Mary and to the Church comes from a single source: Jesus Christ. Mary does not create grace; she receives it. But she receives it in a "preeminent and singular" manner. She is full of grace—full of divine life—to the point of being able, by God's sanctifying will, to truly give it.

One cannot give what one does not have; that much is true. But one certainly can give what one does have—especially if one has received it precisely in order to give it. In her immaculate heart Mary has an untold wealth of grace of which her Son made her the depositary and administrator.

Mary lives in a profound intimacy with God the Father, God the Son, and God the Holy Spirit. As Blessed Josemaría wrote, "Only faith can shed some light on how a creature can be raised to such great heights, becoming a loving target for the delights of the Trinity. We know this is a divine secret. Yet because our Mother is involved, we feel we can understand it more—if we are entitled to speak this way—than other truths of the faith" (1982a: 171). If any good Christian is one with Christ already in this life, and will be much more so in heaven, then in what degree of unity (with no loss of personality; with, in fact, the opposite) must the Virgin Mary now be living? Her relationship with each of the divine Persons seems to reinforce or enrich her relationships with the other two, in a kind of upward spiral which would make us poor sinners dizzy to even contemplate. But she has no problem with vertigo, because she is immersed in Life itself. And that is exactly why if any creature can be called a giver of life, that creature is the Blessed Virgin Mary.

Sanctifying grace is life. It is a mysterious but very real participation in divine life; it is what makes us "born of God" (see 1 Jn 3:9). "You have been born anew," Saint Peter tells us, "not of perishable seed but of imperishable, through the living and abiding word of God" (1 Pt 1:23). By adoption we are God's children. Divine filiation is not ours by nature; we are not born living the life of God. But when we are adopted by God the Father, the Holy Spirit infuses into us a new life of true communion with God in Christ. "If anyone is in Christ, he is a new creature; the old has passed away, behold, the new has come," says Saint Paul (2 Cor 5:17).

Our new life has all the characteristics of created life: conception, gestation, birth, development, maturity. It begins as a fragile seed, a seed easily destroyed by sin, but with careful cultivation it ends up being the robust, indestructible, full-of-God life of the blessed in heaven. This life has its absolute origin in the Blessed Trinity; more specifically, in the Person of the Holy Spirit. In virtue of the hypostatic union, this divine life fills the humanity of Christ the Redeemer, Christ the Head of a new humanity. But, at the very same time, it also fills her who is most marvelously one with him: the Eve who could say of her Adam, "He is bone of my bone and flesh of my flesh."[14]

Actually it is not so surprising, though it is wonderful, that God chose to make the diffusion or multiplication of supernatural life depend not on himself alone, but also on the will of the Mother of the Redeemer. Endowed with a certain relative fullness of grace at the moment of her Immaculate Conception, she was, after all, destined to enjoy from the moment of her Assumption a fullness with no restriction whatsoever.

How often Saint Paul speaks about living the life of Jesus! See, for example, 2 Corinthians 4:10–12, Colossians 3:3–4, and 2 Timothy 3:12. He is talking about a very real life, a life so marvelously vigorous and fruitful that he can honestly claim that "I became your father in Christ Jesus through the Gospel" (1 Cor 4:15), and exclaim, "My little children, with whom I am again in travail until Christ be formed in you!" (Gal 4:19).

Indeed, God's goodness is so great that he wants to give us—each and every one of us, according to our individual capacities—all that he can of himself. God our Father gives us a share in his Fatherhood, making us capable of spiritual procreation; he gives us a share in the filiation of his Son; finally, he gives us a share in the Love that is the Holy Spirit. By grace, every Christian is capable of being a father and a mother, a son and a holy spirit (a "paraclete": advocate, defender, consoler, love) for others.

But this capacity has been given in a qualitatively superior way to the creature who was constituted the Mother of God. Having been assumed body and soul into heaven; enjoying the glorious existence of consummate and eternal beatitude; privileged with the most intimate union with the three divine Persons—what can the Blessed Virgin not do for us now? Before he was conceived in her virginal womb, Christ the Head was conceived in Mary's mind and heart: by the power of the Holy Spirit, through her faith in the word of God (see RM 13). In an analogous way, the members of Christ's Mystical Body, the "other Christs," are also brought to life in Christ by operation of the Holy Spirit in the Immaculate Heart of Mary.

By the will of God, as a great gift from God, Mary is mysteriously involved in the transmission of divine life. Somehow she actively cooperates with the Holy Spirit in the giving of supernatural life, the life of sanctifying grace, that life with Christ which she possesses in superabundant fullness. In his second sermon for the feast of the Assumption, Saint Bernard comments on the fact that the angel Gabriel, at the Annunciation, first saluted Mary as "full of grace" and then "*also* declared that the Holy Ghost was to come upon her" (1984, 173; emphasis added). "To what purpose," he asks, "if it be not to fill her to overflowing? To what purpose, I repeat, except that, being filled in herself by His first coming, she might be made to superabound and overflow unto us by His second? Would to God those spiritual spices, those precious gifts of grace were poured out upon us, so that of so great a fullness we might all receive!"

Pope Paul VI, in *The Credo of the People of God,* affirmed the reality of Mary's "cooperating with the birth and growth of divine life in the souls of the redeemed." And Pope John Paul II has reaffirmed it. In section 47 of *Redemptoris Mater,* for example, he rejoices that at the Second Vatican Council his predecessor "solemnly proclaimed that Mary is the Mother of the Church, 'that is, Mother of the entire Christian people, both faithful and pastors,'" and that later, in *The Credo of the People of God,* Pope Paul made that "even more forceful" restatement of the same proclamation. It is worth noting, by the way, that Mary's spiritual motherhood was "the central recurring theme" in the teaching of Pope John XXIII.[15]

The affirmation in question is really quite a daring one. The spiritual motherhood ascribed to Mary is not a merely honorific position. Nor is it limited to a constant intercession, of admittedly superlative value, before the Blessed Trinity. Mary's intercessory power is, as a matter of fact, rooted in her spiritual motherhood—not vice versa.

We are talking about a cooperation within the life of grace as such: a cooperation which bears upon the very being of that "new" creature "born again" of the Holy Spirit; a cooperation which continually bears upon that creature as it keeps growing in Christian life, the life of Christ, the life of God.

We also have to thank Mary for the fact that, as members of Christ, we can share in both the Fatherhood of God and the motherhood of the Blessed Virgin. As Blessed Josemaría says (*Friends of God*: 281), "If we become identified with Mary and imitate her virtues, we will be able to bring Christ to life, through grace, in the souls of many who will in turn become identified with him through the action of the Holy Spirit. If we imitate Mary, we will share in some way in her spiritual motherhood."

Mary, we repeat, is not the author of grace. But everything leads us to believe that God freely committed himself to making her the true mother of our sanctification, a true giver of supernatural life: that Christocentric life which originates in the Blessed Trinity and comes to us from the Father, in the Son, through the Holy Spirit.

In the natural parent-child relationship, parents have to set limits to promote the healthy development of their children. But in the supernatural parent-child relationship, no such restrictions apply: the order of grace transcends them. When it comes to holiness, there is no such thing as too much or too soon.

Therefore, given God's will, Christ's human will, Christ's glorified state, and the total union of Mary's will (by grace of the Holy Spirit) with that of Christ, her Redeemer and ours, we can say that for God to create supernatural life in a soul, it is enough for Mary to simply will it. Thus, in a spiritual, real, vital, and full sense, Mary is truly "our mother in the order of grace" (LG 61).

Mediatrix to the Mediator

If Mary is our true mother in the order of grace, she is also the mediatrix of all graces. "So great a Mediator is Christ," says Saint Bernard, "that we have need of another to mediate between Him and us, and for this we can find none so well qualified as Mary" (1984, 207). Though *Lumen Gentium* (in section 62) lists "Mediatrix" after three other titles ("Advocate," "Auxiliatrix," and "Adjutrix"), Mary's role as mediatrix is discussed throughout chapter 8 (sections 52–69).

Actually, with respect to Mary, "spiritual motherhood" and "mediation" are complementary terms. For it is precisely as Mother of the Redeemer and Mother of the redeemed that she unites human beings with the Redeemer.

Let us review the deep metaphysical and theological implications of the term "participation." "To participate" means, of course, "to take part." When we take part in a material good—a cake, for example—the more of us that are taking part in it, the less of it each of us gets. But when we take part in spiritual goods like joy and compassion, which are not things or objects, the greater the number of participants, the more there is to go around.

In fact, the more spiritual, the more perfect, the more perfecting is the good, the more it can be shared. The infinite goodness of God, who alone is the Good, is the cause of innumerable goods, both spiritual and material. These lesser goods are created, limited, finite, but nevertheless true goods. Goodness is, in other words, naturally generous. And this rule applies even more, rather than less, to the spiritual realm than to the material realm.

Christ's role as mediator is a prime example. He is the one and only "born" mediator, the one capital-M Mediator, because in his person, and only in his person, divine nature is hypostatically united with human nature. But for that very reason he can give us a share in his mediation, since we have both human nature and a real participation, through grace, in the divine life of the Blessed Trinity. Such sharing "in no way obscures or diminishes this unique mediation of Christ, but rather shows its power" (LG 60). Indeed, it only makes more manifest the richness, the consistency, and the supreme dignity of the unique mediation of Christ.

There is no problem with calling others mediators between God and mankind, in a certain sense: namely, insofar as they cooperate, in a dependent and subordinate way, in Christ's work of uniting people with God. We can and should facilitate that union, that work of Christ's, by being instruments he can use for that purpose—in much the same way as do the angels and the saints, the prophets and the priests, of both Testaments.

Certainly "no creature could ever be counted as equal with the Incarnate Word and Redeemer." Nevertheless, "just as the priesthood of Christ is shared in various ways both by the ministers and by the faithful, and as the one goodness of God is really communicated in different ways to His creatures, so also the unique mediation of the Redeemer does not exclude but rather gives rise to a manifold cooperation which is but a sharing in this one source" (LG 62). In other words, the uniqueness of Christ's mediation does not rule out reciprocity and collaboration between him and us. Such is the goodness of our God that all of us can in many different ways be for one another, in communion with our Savior, mediators before God. The Second Vatican Council said this with regard to Mary, but it is true of all of us: every Christian has a "salvific influence" on others that "originates, not from some inner necessity, but from the divine pleasure. It flows forth from the superabundance of the merits of Christ, rests on His mediation, depends entirely on it and draws all its power from it. In no way does it impede, but rather does it foster the immediate union of the faithful with Christ" (LG 60).

All this refers to men and women in general and therefore to Mary. But Mary's mediation takes on an extraordinary, unrepeatable character. Just as there is an essential distinction between the common priesthood of the faithful and the ministerial priesthood, there is also an essential difference between our mediation and that of Mary. No matter how perfect or intense is our participation in Christ's mediation, it will never attain the degree of Mary's since she alone is the Mother of God. Anyone else's mediation can only be filial. Except, that is, in the case of priests, when they act *in persona Christi*, but then again, being the Mother of the Mediator is qualitatively superior to making Christ present on the altar. Thus we understand this affirmation from Pope John Paul: "Mary's mediation *is intimately linked with her motherhood*. It possesses a specifically maternal character, which distinguishes it from the mediation of the other creatures" (RM 38).

Mediatrix of all graces

In the Blessed Virgin Mary, says Saint Bernard, God "has placed the plenitude of all good; so that if there is anything of hope in us, if anything of grace, if anything of salvation, we may feel assured it has overflowed unto us from her. . . . Therefore, my dearest brethren, with every fiber, every feeling of our hearts, with all the affections of our minds, and with all the ardor of our souls, let us honor Mary, because such is the will of God, who would have us to obtain everything through the hands of Mary" (1984, 85–86).

Pope Leo XIII, in his encyclical *Octobri Mense* (see OL 113), sanctions the belief that Mary mediates and dispenses all graces:

> She was the representative of all mankind, according to the illustrious and learned opinion of Saint Thomas, who says that "in the Annunciation was awaited the consent of the Virgin standing in the place of humanity" (ST III.30.1). With equal truth it may be said that of the great treasury of all graces

given to us by our Lord—'for grace and truth came by Jesus Christ' (Jn 1:17)—nothing comes to us except through the mediation of Mary, for such is the will of God. Thus, as no man goes to the Father but by the Son, so no one goes to Christ except through His Mother.

Her intercessory role

Redemptoris Mater develops the intercessory aspect of Mary's mediation for the good of all her children; and does so on the basis of the Gospel account of the wedding feast in Cana of Galilee that the Mother of Jesus attended. *"She puts herself 'in the middle,'* that is to say, *she acts as a Mediatrix not as an outsider, but in her position as mother.* She knows that as such she can point out to her Son the needs of mankind, and in fact, she 'has the right' to do so. Her mediation is thus in the nature of intercession: Mary 'intercedes' for mankind" (RM 21).

God wanted us to have an advocate in heaven worthy of always being heard. He wanted Mary who is *gratia plena sibi* [full of grace herself] to be also *superplena nobis* [more than full of grace for us], as Saint Bernard said. From her Son, the Author of all grace, the Mother of God was given all grace to be *Administratrix Christi* on our behalf. In his encyclical, *Iucunda Semper* (see OL 155), Pope Leo XIII affirms "that law of merciful mediation . . . which Saint Bernadine of Siena thus expresses: 'Every grace granted to man has three successive steps: By God it is communicated to Christ, from Christ it passes to the Virgin, and from the Virgin it descends to us.'" This wonder is yet another manifestation of God's immense love for Mary and for us. To put all supernatural wealth in the hands of a mother like his was to give everyone in the world a most precious gift: the assurance of a welcome into heaven for anyone who faithfully and conscientiously has recourse to this most gentle and merciful of mothers. As the moon softly reflects the light of the sun, the Blessed Virgin particularly reflects the mercy of God. This is the Mother of God and our mother, the ultimate extreme of God's love and wisdom for us creatures who are in need of understanding, compassion, forgiveness, salvation, and life with God.

Mary's formational mission

"Another essential element of Mary's maternal task is found in her words to the servants: 'Do whatever he tells you.' The Mother of Christ presents herself as the spokeswoman of her Son's will, pointing out those things which must be done so that the salvific power of the Messiah may be manifested. At Cana, thanks to the intercession of Mary and the obedience of the servants, Jesus begins 'his hour.' At Cana Mary appears as believing in Jesus. Her faith evokes his first 'sign' and helps to kindle the faith of the disciples" (RM 21).

Mary's protective mission

Let us, this one time, take a testimony to the Christian faith from the pen of a nonecclesiastical writer: Miguel de Cervantes. In book one, chapter six of his novel *The Trials of Persiles and Sigismunda: A Northern Story*, a "barbarian woman" offers this detailed proof that she is really a normal, decent, civilized person:

> "[My husband] explained as much of his religion to me as he knows and I gave it a place in my heart and soul where I've accepted it with all the belief I can. I believe in the Holy Trinity, God the Father, God the Son, and God the Holy Spirit, three separate persons who are all the one true God and, although they're God the Father, God the Son, and God the Holy Spirit, they're not three distinct and separate gods but the one true God. Finally, I believe in everything the Holy Roman Catholic Church holds to and believes, for it is ruled by the Holy Spirit and governed by the Supreme Pontiff, vicar

and viceroy of God on earth, legitimate successor to Saint
Peter, its first shepherd after Christ, who in turn is first and
universal shepherd of his wife the Church. He told me of the
greatness of the perpetual Virgin Mary, Queen of Heaven and
Our Lady and Lady of the Angels, treasure of the Father, sanc-
tuary of the Son, and beloved of the Holy Spirit, help and
refuge of sinners."

Certainly our popes have often encouraged confidence in
Mary as refuge of sinners,[16] but this passage from Cervantes shows
with striking clarity how deeply ingrained in Christian conscious-
ness that confidence is.

Mary's spiritual motherhood is not limited to the moment in
which a soul is first given the life of grace. How can our most holy
mother fail to be an ongoing refuge for us, her children, when she
sees in each of us her precious Son, whether glorified by grace or
crucified by sin? "This maternity of Mary in the order of grace,"
the Second Vatican Council clearly stated, "began with the consent
which she gave in faith at the Annunciation and which she sustained without wavering beneath the cross, and lasts until the eternal fulfillment of the elect. Taken up to heaven she did not lay
aside this salvific duty, but by her constant intercession continued
to bring us the gifts of eternal salvation. . . . Therefore the Blessed
Virgin is invoked in the Church under the title of Advocate . . ."
(LG 62).

Mary's love

In a study such as this, we should approach the subject of Mary's
love for her children not simply from the perspective of our own
personal experiences of that love, but also in a more formal way.

The moment we do that, we find ourselves confronting an
unfathomable mystery, one accessible only to God and Mary: she

loves us in the Holy Spirit. In a homily given on May 13, 1982, during a pilgrimage to Portugal, Pope John Paul touched upon this mystery. "Mary," he said, "embraces us all with special solicitude in the Holy Spirit, for as we profess in our Creed, he is 'the giver of life.' It is he who gives the fullness of life, open toward eternity. Mary's spiritual motherhood is, therefore, a sharing in the power of the Holy Spirit, of 'the giver of life.' It is the humble service of her who says of herself: 'Behold, I am the handmaid of the Lord.'"[17]

"God only counts to one!" André Frossard is reported to have said, and the same is true of Mary. Mary, like any good mother, loves each of her children as if that son or daughter were her only child. As Pope John Paul says, "Of the essence of motherhood is the fact that it concerns the person. Motherhood always establishes a unique and unrepeatable relationship between two people: between mother and child and between child and mother. Even when the same woman is the mother of many children, her personal relationship with each one of them is of the very essence of motherhood. For each child is generated in a unique and unrepeatable way, and this is true both for the mother and for the child. Each child is surrounded in the same way by that maternal love on which are based the child's development and coming to maturity as a human being" (RM 45).

1. Daughters of St. Paul 1979, 253.
2. See CA 41 and SR 38–40.
3. GS 22, as quoted in RH 13.
4. *The Grace of Christ and Original Sin* 2.24.28: see FEF 3:1857.
5. "Put on the Lord Jesus Christ!": OR 9/5/83.
6. FEF 1:217a; see also Kelly 1960, 172.
7. FEF 1:248; emphasis added.
8. See O'Carroll 1983, 253; Scheeben 2:69; FEF 2:1020a.
9. See FEF 3:1578, 1644, 2133; ND 606/10.
10. LG 56; see also RM 19.

11. Josemaría Escrivá, *The Forge,* 234.
12. See Col 1:24 and MCo: OL 384.
13. See ID: St. Paul edition, p. 15.
14. See Papali 1987, 38.
15. See O'Carroll 1983, 255–56.
16. See OL, pp. 547–48, and RM 11, 24, 27.
17. "Mary's Maternal Love": TPS 27:242.

7. Cult of the Blessed Virgin Mary

CULT IS AN HONOR we render to a being that is superior to ourselves. To honor a servant of God is to honor God himself, who manifests himself in his servants and who thus attracts us to himself. As the Council of Trent explicitly stated, it is not superstitious to believe "that the saints enjoying eternal happiness in heaven are to be invoked." In fact, we can and should "have recourse to [the saints'] prayers, to their help and assistance, in order to obtain favors from God through His Son, our Lord Jesus Christ, who alone is our Redeemer and Savior" (ND 1255).

For many reasons, it is only right that our Lady should be the object of a most singular veneration. She is, after all, as Saint Peter Damian so beautifully expressed it, "the fount of the living fount."[1] It is, as Pope Pius XII explained, entirely appropriate that "the Virgin Mary, Mother of God, is the recipient of a more exalted worship. Because of the function she received from God, her life is closely linked with the mysteries of Christ, and no one assuredly has followed more closely and effectively in the steps of the Incarnate Word; no one enjoys greater favor and greater power with the Sacred Heart of the Son of God and, through Him, with His heavenly Father."[2]

In placing his mother at the very apex of holiness, in constantly filling her with overflowing graces, God expresses his will that we honor her as much as is humanly possible. For to praise Mary is to praise her Son and, through him, the Father and the Holy Spirit. What son is not happy to see his mother honored? And how much more Christ loves his mother than anyone else in the world loves theirs! How well we understand that woman's shout of praise for Jesus' mother: "Blessed is the womb that bore you, and the breasts that you sucked!" (Lk 11:27). Those blessings recorded in Luke 11:27–28 form the beginning of a chain of praises that will resound, uninterrupted, through the ages. Mary herself foretold this. "Behold," she said, "henceforth all generations will call me blessed; for he who is mighty has done great things for me, and holy is his name" (Lk 1:48–49). No good son or daughter of God would, then, refuse to join this immense choir which praises God in the way that is nearest and dearest to the heart of his Son: that is, by praising his mother, who is our mother as well.

Mary is, said the Second Vatican Council, "justly honored by a special cult in the Church. . . . This cult, as it has always existed, although it is altogether singular, differs essentially from the cult of adoration which is offered to the Incarnate Word, as well as to the Father and the Holy Spirit, and it is most favorable to it" (LG 66). In classic Church terminology, this type of veneration that belongs uniquely to Mary is called *hyperdulia*. Saint Thomas explains: "Since *latria* [adoration] is due to God alone, . . . [and] the Blessed Virgin is a mere rational creature, the worship of *latria* is not due to her, but only that of *dulia* [high honor]: but in a higher degree than to other creatures, inasmuch as she is the Mother of God. For this reason we say that not [just] any kind of *dulia* is due to her, but *hyperdulia*" (ST III.25.5; cf. LG 66).

Liturgical celebrations

Echoing Pope Paul VI (MCu 56), the *Catechism* declares that "'the Church's devotion to the Blessed Virgin is intrinsic to Christian worship'" (CCC 971). Since, as the Second Vatican Council said, it is "in the liturgy" that "the whole public worship is performed by the Mystical Body of Christ," and since "from this it follows that every liturgical celebration . . . is a sacred action surpassing all others" (SC 7), the fact that in many liturgical celebrations "holy Church honors with especial love the Blessed Mary, Mother of God . . ." (see SC 102–103) calls for some clarification.

Acknowledging that "it is the custom of the Church occasionally to celebrate some Masses in honor and remembrance of the saints," the Council of Trent explained this custom as follows: "The Church teaches that sacrifice is offered not to the saints, but to God alone who has given them their crown. Therefore, 'the priest does not say: "I offer the sacrifice to you, Peter and Paul"'; but, giving thanks to God for the victory of the saints, he implores their protection 'in order that those whose remembrance we celebrate on earth may intercede for us in heaven'" (ND 1549). If this is true with regard to all the saints, then, as the Second Vatican Council pointed out, it is particularly true with regard to ". . . the Blessed Mary, Mother of God, who is joined by an inseparable bond to the saving work of her Son" (SC 103).

In the revised list of feasts drawn up by the post-Vatican II Consilium, as summarized by Father O'Carroll (1983, 223), "fourteen feasts are of our Lord, but five of these (the *Annunciation,* the *Nativity,* the *Epiphany,* the *Holy Family,* and the *Presentation*) involve Mary. Of her feasts, thirteen still remain. . . . Three are solemnities: *The Mother of God* (now January 1 . . .); the *Immaculate Conception*; and the *Assumption.* Two, the *Nativity* [of Mary] and the *Visitation,* have festive rank. Three are ordinary *memoriae*: the *Presentation* [of our Lady]; *Our Lady Queen*; and *Our Lady of the Rosary.* . . . The remaining four are optional: *Our Lady of Mount Carmel*; *Our Lady of Lourdes*; the *Immaculate Heart of Mary* . . . ; and *Our Lady of the Snows* (Dedication of the Basilica of St. Mary Major). The Saturday Mass of Our Lady still remains and, as Paul VI pointed out in *Marialis Cultus,* is now more frequently available. The Pope also reminded us that local calendars may add to the list of the Roman Missal; this no longer has Masses for local celebration."

Marian devotions

Seeking to correct what they viewed as excesses of Marian piety, Erasmus, Luther and even John Calvin asserted that true devotion to Mary consists in imitating her (see O'Carroll 1983, 94). In a more nuanced and profound way, the Second Vatican Council said much the same thing: "True devotion consists neither in sterile or transitory affection, nor in a certain vain credulity, but proceeds from true faith, by which we are led to know the excellence of the Mother of God, and we are moved to a filial love toward our mother and to the imitation of her virtues" (LG 67).

Pope Paul VI, in 1974, wrote an apostolic exhortation on the subject of Marian devotion: *Marialis Cultus*. In this document he clarified and explained traditional forms of Marian piety which were often overshadowed by liturgical or disciplinary changes in the Church and also frequently undervalued by religious commentators in the post-conciliar period.

Well aware that, as Pope Paul said at the beginning of *Marialis Cultus,* "the liturgy has an incomparable pastoral effectiveness and a recognized exemplary value for the other forms of worship," the Second Vatican Council urged that "the cult, especially the liturgical cult, of the Blessed Virgin be generously fostered" (LG 67). But it also pointed out that "the sacred liturgy does not exhaust the entire activity of the Church" (SC 9). "The spiritual life," said the Council, "is not limited solely to participation in the liturgy. The Christian is indeed called to pray with his brethren, but he must also enter into his chamber to pray to the Father, in secret (cf. Mt 6:6); yet more, according to the teaching of the Apostle, he should pray without ceasing (cf. 1 Thes 5:17)" (SC 12).

The Council explicitly urged that "the practices and exercises of piety recommended by the magisterium of the Church toward [Mary] in the course of centuries be made of great moment" (LG 67). In keeping with that spirit, Pope Paul VI in 1965 wrote an encyclical, *Mense Maio,* on prayers to be offered during the month of May for the preservation of peace. That encyclical includes the following exhortation: "Do not fail to put repeated emphasis on the recitation of the Rosary, the prayer so pleasing to our Lady and so often recommended by the Roman Pontiffs. It affords the faithful an excellent means of complying effectively and pleasingly with our divine Master's command: 'Ask, and it shall be given to you; seek, and you shall find; knock, and it shall be opened to you'" (MM 14: Carlen 1981, 163).

Other practices of Marian piety

The Second Vatican Council "deliberately teaches" the "Catholic doctrine" that "the various forms of piety toward the Mother of God, which the Church within the limits of sound and orthodox doctrine, according to the conditions of time and place, and the nature and ingenuity of the faithful has approved, bring it about that while the Mother is honored, the Son, through whom all things have their being (cf. Col 1:15–16) and in whom it has pleased the Father that all fullness should dwell (cf. Col 1:19), is rightly known, loved and glorified and that all His commands are observed" (LG 66–67). These various forms include Saturday and Month of May devotions; participation in Marian confraternities, associations, and congresses; pilgrimages to Marian shrines; the use of icons and holy cards; the wearing of medals; and the Scapular of Mount Carmel.

Fruits of devotion to the Blessed Virgin

Devotion to the Blessed Virgin brings us, both individually and collectively, many blessings. Here are but a few:

• *Unity with Christ.* "Who more than His Mother could have a far-reaching knowledge of the admirable mysteries of the birth and childhood of Christ, and above all of the mystery of the Incarnation, which is the beginning and the foundation of faith? . . . Sharing as she did the thoughts and the secret wishes of Christ, she may be said to have lived the very life of her Son. . . . Hence . . . the Blessed Virgin is more powerful than all others as a means of uniting mankind with Christ. In fact, if, as Christ said, 'Now this is eternal life: That they may know Thee, the Only True God, and Jesus Christ, whom Thou hast sent' (Jn 17:3), and if through Mary we attain to the knowledge of Christ, through Mary also we most easily obtain that life of which Christ is the source and origin" (AD: OL 227–28). "Mary, who since her entry into salvation history unites in herself and re-echoes the greatest teachings of the faith as she is proclaimed and venerated, calls the faithful to her Son and His sacrifice and to the love of the Father" (LG 65).

• *Attraction to the Eucharist.* "The piety of the Christian people has always very rightly sensed a profound link between devotion to the Blessed Virgin and worship of the Eucharist: this is a fact that can be seen in the liturgy of both the West and the East, in the traditions of the Religious Families, in the modern movements of spirituality, including those for youth, and in the pastoral practice of the Marian Shrines. Mary guides the faithful to the Eucharist" (RM 44).

• *Confidence.* "No one can meditate upon [the mysteries of the rosary] without feeling a new awakening in his heart of confidence that he will certainly obtain through Mary the fullness of the mercies of God" (IS: OL 154). "While on one hand Mary is all powerful with her divine Son who grants all graces to mankind through her, on the other hand she is by nature so good and so merciful that inclined to aid spontaneously those who suffer she is absolutely incapable of refusing her help to those who invoke her" (FA: OL 275).

• *Protection from evil.* "Guided by her they [the faithful] will not go astray; aided by her prayer they will not despair; protected by her they will be safe" (SQ: OL 18). "The hope of salvation can never be absent whenever hearts are turned with sincere and ardent piety to the most holy Mother of God. . . . When Mary interposes her powerful protection, the gates of hell cannot prevail" (SV: OL 574).

• *Moral inspiration and guidance.* "Mary is the radiant sign and inviting model of the moral life. As Saint Ambrose put it, 'The life of this one person can serve as a model for everyone' and while speaking specifically to virgins but within a context open to all, he affirmed: 'The first stimulus to learning is the nobility of the teacher. Who can be more noble than the Mother of God? Who can be more glorious than the one chosen by Glory itself?'" (VS 120).

1. See O'Carroll 1983, 285.
2. MeD: OL 440; see also OL, pp. 544–45.

8. *The Eminent Holiness of Saint Joseph*

THAT SAINT JOSEPH is the greatest saint after Mary is today a generally accepted teaching. In 1870 Pope Pius IX officially declared Saint Joseph to be the Patron of the Universal Church. With reference to that decree, Pope John Paul says in *Redemptoris Custos,* his encyclical on Saint Joseph, that "for Pius IX this was no idle gesture, since by virtue of the sublime dignity which God has granted to his most faithful servant Joseph, 'the Church, after the Blessed Virgin, his spouse, has always held him in great honor and showered him with praise, having recourse to him amid tribulations'" (RC 28).

In 1889 Pope Leo XIII, in *Quamquam Pluries* (his encyclical on Saint Joseph), said that the "special motives" for which Pope Pius IX had made that proclamation, "and for which the Church looks for singular benefit from [Saint Joseph's] patronage and protection," are "that Joseph was the spouse of Mary and that he was the putative father of Jesus Christ." He then gives this explanation (QP: PDM 47–48):

> As Joseph has been united to the Blessed Virgin by the ties of marriage, it may not be doubted that *he approached nearer than anyone else to the eminent dignity by which the Mother of God so nobly surpasses all created natures.* . . . In giving Joseph the Blessed Virgin as spouse, God appointed him to be, not only her life's companion, the witness of her virginity, the protector of her honor, but also, *by virtue of the conjugal tie, a participator in her sublime dignity.*

It is, in fact, as Father Francis Filas says (1962, 381), "becoming more and more commonly accepted in the Church" that Saint Joseph "surpasses all creatures except Mary in holiness." On this subject Pope John Paul, in *Redemptoris Custos,* simply quotes Pope

Leo: "'There can be no doubt but that Joseph approached as no other person ever could that eminent dignity whereby the Mother of God towers above all creatures.'" In order to come closer than any other human being to the "eminent dignity" whereby Mary "towers above all creatures," Saint Joseph need not be higher than the angels. Nevertheless, there are serious theological grounds for believing that he is.[1]

One such consideration is that that "most august dignity" spoken of by Pope Leo is rooted in Saint Joseph's "connection with the hypostatic union, whereby the divine and human nature of our Lord were linked in the one divine Person of the Second Person of the Trinity" (Filas 1962, 607). Pope Pius XI, in several discourses, developed this theme. Here are a few excerpts, as quoted by Father Filas:

> "[Saint Joseph's] was a unique and magnificent mission, that of protecting the Son of God and King of the world; the mission of protecting the virginity and holiness of Mary; the singular mission of entering into participation in the great mystery hidden from the eyes of past ages, and of thus cooperating in the Incarnation and in the Redemption" (p. 607).

> "It is in the grandeur of this mission that the singular and absolutely incomparable holiness of Saint Joseph lies, because truly such a great mission was not confided to any other soul, to any other saint, and thus, between Joseph and God we do not see nor can we see anyone except the most holy Mary with her divine maternity" (p. 606).

> "We are in the order of the hypostatic union, of the personal union of God with man. . . . In the case of Jesus and of Mary, the angels offer them respect and veneration. And in their turn, Jesus and Mary themselves obey and offer their homage to Joseph, for they reverence what the hand of God has established in him, namely, the authority of spouse and the authority of father" (p. 608).

Blessed Josemaría Escrivá, who had a great devotion to Saint Joseph, very much liked "to address him affectionately as 'our father and lord.'" Saint Joseph, he explained, "really is a father and lord," for the following reasons: "He was a man ever faithful to the mission God gave him. . . . He protects those who revere him and accompanies them on their journey through this life—just as he protected and accompanied Jesus when he was growing up. As you get to know him, you discover that the holy patriarch is also a master of the interior life—for he teaches us to know Jesus and share our life with him, and to realize that we are part of God's family. Saint Joseph can teach us these lessons, because he is an ordinary man, a family man, a worker who earned his living by manual labor—all of which has great significance and is a source of happiness for us" (*Christ Is Passing By*: 39). "Saint Joseph, our father and lord, is a teacher of the interior life. Put yourself under his patronage and you'll feel the effect of his power" (*The Way*: 560).

Saint Joseph's doubt

The Gospel accounts seem to imply that after the Annunciation the Blessed Virgin kept to herself the great mystery within her: that of the Incarnation of the Word. There were, after all, no words to really express it. Nor did God seem to want her to reveal it, even to Saint Joseph. However, when Mary arrives at Elizabeth's house, it immediately becomes obvious that Elizabeth has already been informed. "Why is this granted me," she asks, "that the mother of my Lord should come to me?" (Lk 1:43).

How did Elizabeth know? Had Mary and Joseph previously spoken to her? Had the angel's revelation to Joseph already taken place? Did Joseph go with Mary to visit Elizabeth? The Gospel texts do not answer these questions. Moreover, the standard translations do not make it easy to ascertain Joseph's feelings and attitude.

"Now the birth of Jesus Christ took place in this way. When

his mother Mary had been betrothed to Joseph, before they came together she was found to be with child of the Holy Spirit; and her husband Joseph, being a *just man* and unwilling to *put her to shame,* resolved to *send her away* quietly" (Mt 1:18–19 [RSV]). The italicized phrases present us with a real problem. What exactly is being said here?

The key to solving this problem is linguistic analysis of the Greek words here translated as "just man," "put her to shame," and "send her away": dikaïos, deïgmatisaï, and apolusaï. Father Ignace de la Potterie, in *Mary in the Mystery of the Covenant,* provides a most helpful analysis of these words.

• *Dikaïos.* "The best translation of this word," he says, "is 'just.' But the question which poses itself is to know in what sense Joseph is called 'just.' For certain authors, this means that Joseph wished to observe rigorously the Jewish Law. Now according to this law, a woman who had committed adultery must not only be condemned, but stoned" (p. 40). An interpretation which would make better sense in this context is " 'just before God.' Not in the strict sense of a meticulous observation of the Jewish Law, but of a total respect for the will of God and for His action in our lives. . . . We could thus describe the attitude of Joseph: 'God is here at work, I must let him act; I must take myself away from this.' Thus it is out of respect and in religious awe before the mystery of God that Joseph wishes to remove himself" (p. 40).

• *Deïgmatisaï.* The infinitive *deïgmatizô* "derives from the root-verb *deïknumi,* which signifies to show, to indicate, to point out." *Deïgmatizô,* therefore, "can mean simply 'to make known,' 'to bring to light,' without any pejorative connotation. That such a meaning sometimes applies depends uniquely on that which one makes known" (p. 41).

• *Apolusaï.* "The verb *luô* means 'to detach,' 'to unbind.' *Apoluô,* which is derived from it, can simply mean 'to let free,' 'to let go,' but it could also have the meaning 'to send back'; this is said of 'undoing, or breaking the bonds of marriage.'" At least in Matthew 1:19, however, *apoluô* "cannot mean 'to divorce,' . . . since divorce is a public act, in front of witnesses, while here the verb is accompanied by the adverb 'secretly'" (p. 42).

Father de la Potterie would translate verse 19 thus: "Joseph, her spouse, who was a just man and who did not wish to unveil (her mystery), resolved to secretly separate himself from her" (pp. 54–55). There are, as he demonstrates, sound exegetical reasons to believe that Joseph already knew what had happened to Mary, and that the person he had doubts about was not her but himself.

We arrive, then, at the same conclusion as did several of the Church Fathers. To quote just one, Saint Ephraim of Syria, "Joseph understood that this was an admirable work of God. . . . But he thought especially of sending her away so as not to commit a sin in allowing himself to be called father of the Savior. He feared to live with her lest he dishonor the name of the Virgin's Son. That is why the angel said to him, 'Do not fear to take Mary to your home'" (O'Carroll 1983, 123–24). Saint Joseph is, in other words, the just man par excellence.

And for that very reason the angel does not simply confirm the divine origin of Mary's pregnancy. Joseph himself, he is told, has a vital connection to this mystery: "You shall call his name Jesus." This is the announcement of Joseph's great mission to be the legal father of Jesus.

Saint Joseph's fatherhood

But was Joseph's fatherhood just a legal formality? Far from it. As Father Filas points out (1962, 159–60), the Gospel contains "various references to the authoritative position of Saint Joseph"— Luke 2:22, Luke 2:51, and Matthew 2:13–23, for example— which "lead to the conclusion that he exercises over Jesus a certain right as a father."

In section 7 of *Redemptoris Custos,* Pope John Paul identifies Joseph's marriage to Mary as "the juridical basis of his fatherhood" and makes it clear that this is no mere technicality. "The Son of Mary," says the Holy Father, "is also Joseph's Son by virtue of the marriage bond that unites them: 'By reason of their faithful marriage both of them deserve to be called Christ's parents, not only his mother, but also his father, who was a parent in the same way that he was the mother's spouse: in mind, not in the flesh.'" In a homily given at Terni (Italy) on March 19, 1981, Pope John Paul included this magnificent tribute: "Joseph ... reflects in his person, more than any other human father, the fatherhood of God himself."[2]

Obviously Joseph is not Jesus' father in the same sense that Mary is his mother. But his parenthood is, like hers, virginal. As Saint Augustine says, "We should count [the genealogy] through Joseph, because as he was virginally the husband, so was he virginally the father. . . ."[3] We should indeed, as Pope John Paul said at Terni, "venerate Joseph who built a family home on earth for the eternal Word of God, just as Mary had given the Word a human body" (TPS 26: 177). For, as Pope Leo pointed out, "the divine household which Joseph ruled with the authority of a father contained within its limits the beginnings of the Church" (QP: PDM 48).

St. Joseph's privileges and recognition

Joseph has been called by classical Spanish authors: "Nurturer of the Creator," "Provider of divine Providence," "Crib who rocks God," "Brazier of Love to Warm Him," "Soft Bed Where He Sleeps," "Tree under which God rejoices," "Tree to Shelter God," "Redeemer of Jesus, his Liberator and Savior"(recalling the flight into Egypt), "Rest of Jesus and Mary," "Sweet Refuge of Jesus and Mary," "Guardian Angel of Jesus and Mary." All of these titles reflect in rather poetic language some of the privileges which Joseph enjoyed as the legal father and protector of Jesus.

A liturgical feast day was set aside for Saint Joseph by Sixtus IV in 1476; Innocent VIII raised it to a higher category in 1486. Then Gregory XV declared the feast a universal holy day of obligation in 1621. In 1870, the First Vatican Council proposed Saint Joseph as Patron of the Universal Church, but the document couldn't be signed. However, Pius IX, who had proclaimed the Immaculate Conception as a dogma, acknowledged the title on December 8, 1871.

Pope John XXIII included Saint Joseph in the Roman Canon of the Mass, and Pope John Paul II, in his apostolic exhortation *Redemptoris Custos*, has gathered together patristic and theological tradition and opened new horizons for study and meditation.

1. See Filas 1962, 381–398.
2. "Family Stability and Respect for Life": TPS 26: 177.
3. *Sermones* 51: Filas 1962, 187.

Abbreviations

AC   *Ad Caeli Reginam,* encyclical, Pope Pius XII, October 11, 1954

AD   *Ad Diem Illum,* encyclical, Pope Saint Pius X, February 2, 1904

AP   *Adiutricem Populi,* encyclical, Pope Leo XIII, September 5, 1895

CA   *Centesimus Annus,* encyclical, Pope John Paul II, May 1, 1991

CCC   *Catechism of the Catholic Church*

CIN   Catholic Information Network

DM   *Dives in Misericordia,* encyclical, Pope John Paul II, November 30, 1980

DT   *Diuturni Temporis,* encyclical, Pope Leo XIII, September 5, 1898

DV   *Dei Verbum,* Second Vatican Council Dogmatic Constitution on Divine Revelation

EV   *Evangelium Vitae,* encyclical, Pope John Paul II, March 25, 1995

FA   *Fausto Appetente Die,* encyclical, Pope Benedict XV, June 29, 1921

FEF   *The Faith of the Early Fathers* (Jurgens)

FCon   *Familiaris Consortio,* apostolic exhortation, Pope John Paul II, November 22, 1981

FCor   *Fulgens Corona,* encyclical, Pope Pius XII, September 8, 1953

GS   *Gaudium et Spes,* Second Vatican Council Pastoral Constitution on the Church in the Modern World

HA   *Haurietis Aquas,* encyclical, Pope Pius XII, May 15, 1956

ID   *Ineffabilis Deus,* apostolic constitution, Pope Pius IX, December 8, 1854

IS   *Iucunda Semper,* encyclical, Pope Leo XIII, September 8, 1894

LG   *Lumen Gentium,* Second Vatican Council Dogmatic Constitution on the Church

LV   *Lux Veritatis,* encyclical, Pope Pius XI, December 25, 1931

MCo   *Mystici Corporis,* encyclical, Pope Pius XII, June 29, 1943

MCu   *Marialis Cultus,* apostolic exhortation, Pope Paul VI, February 2, 1974

MD   *Munificentissimus Deus,* apostolic constitution, Pope Pius XII, November 1, 1950

MeD   *Mediator Dei,* encyclical, Pope Pius XII, November 20, 1947

MM   *Mense Maio,* encyclical, Pope Paul VI, April 29, 1965

ND   Neuner and Dupuis, *The Christian Faith*

OL   *Our Lady*

OM   *Octobri Mense,* encyclical, Pope Leo XIII, September 22, 1891

OR   *L'Osservatore Romano,* English edition

PC   *Perfectae Caritatis,* Second Vatican Council Decree on the Renewal of Religious Life

PDM   *Papal Documents on Mary* (Doheny and Kelly)

QP   *Quamquam Pluries,* encyclical, Pope Leo XIII, August 15, 1889

RC   *Redemptoris Custos,* apostolic exhortation, Pope John Paul II, August 15, 1989

RH   *Redemptor Hominis,* encyclical, Pope John Paul II, March 4, 1979

RM   *Redemptoris Mater,* encyclical, Pope John Paul II, March 25, 1987

SA   *Superiore Anno,* letter from Pope Pius XII to Cardinal Luigi Maglione, April 15, 1940

SC   *Sacrosanctum Concilium,* Second Vatican Council, Constitution on the Sacred Liturgy

SQ   *Summa Quidem Animi,* letter from Pope Gregory XVI to the Archbishop of Prague and to the Bishops of Bohemia, April 23, 1845

SR   *Sollicitudo Rei Socialis,* encyclical, Pope John Paul II, December 30, 1987

ST   *Summa Theologiae* (Saint Thomas Aquinas)

SV   *Sacro Vergente Anno,* apostolic letter from Pope Pius XII to the People of Russia, July 7, 1952

TPS   *The Pope Speaks* (journal)

VS   *Veritatis Splendor,* encyclical, Pope John Paul II, August 6, 1993

References

Except where otherwise noted in the text, the translation used for all papal and conciliar documents is the official one provided by the Vatican Press via the Daughters of St. Paul and the United States Catholic Conference. All biblical quotations, except where otherwise noted, are from the Revised Standard Version, Catholic Edition, published by Scepter. Numbers cited refer to content divisions, for sources thus organized; in other cases, they refer to page numbers.

Aquinas, Saint Thomas. 1981. *Summa Theologica.* Complete English edition in five volumes. Trans. Fathers of the English Dominican Province. Allen, Tex.: Christian Classics.

_____. 1990. *The Three Greatest Prayers: Commentaries on the Lord's Prayer, the Hail Mary, and the Apostles' Creed.* Trans. Laurence Shapcote, O.P. Manchester, N.H.: Sophia Institute.

Berard, Aram, S.J., ed. 1991. *History, Science, Theology and the Shroud: Symposium Proceedings.* St. Louis: The Man of the Shroud Committee of Amarillo.

Bernard, Saint. 1984. *St. Bernard's Sermons on the Blessed Virgin Mary.* Trans. from the original Latin by "A Priest of Mount Melleray." Chulmleigh, Devon: Augustine Publishing Co.

Brown, David O., O.S.M., ed. 1990. *Marian Reflections: The Angelus Messages of Pope John Paul II.* Washington, N.J.: AMI Press.

Carlen, Claudia, I.H.M. 1981. *The Papal Encyclicals 1958–1981.* Raleigh, N.C.: McGrath Publishing Co.

Carol, Juniper B., O.F.M. 1956. *Fundamentals of Mariology.* New York: Benziger Brothers.

Catechism of the Catholic Church. 1994. Libreria Editrice Vaticana. San Francisco: Ignatius Press.

Cervantes, Miguel de. 1989. *The Trials of Persiles and Sigismunda: A Northern Story.* Trans. from the Spanish by Celia Richmond Weller and Clark A. Colahan. Berkeley: University of California Press.

Daughters of St. Paul, comps. 1979. *Truth: Messages of John Paul II.* Vol. 2. Boston: Daughters of St. Paul.

Deiss, Lucien, C.S.Sp. 1972. *Mary, Daughter of Sion.* Trans. Barbara T. Blair. Collegeville, Minn.: The Liturgical Press.

de la Potterie, Ignace. 1992. *Mary in the Mystery of the Covenant.* Trans. Bertrand Buby, S.M. New York: Alba House.

Doheny, William J., C.S.C., and Joseph P. Kelly, S.T.D., comps. 1954. *Papal Documents on Mary.* Milwaukee: The Bruce Publishing Co.

Escrivá, Josemaría. 1982a. *Christ Is Passing By.* New Rochelle, N.Y.: Scepter Press.

_____. 1982b. *The Way.* Princeton, N.J.: Scepter Publishers.

_____. 1986. *Friends of God.* New Rochelle, N.Y.: Scepter Press.

_____. 1987. *The Forge.* Princeton, N.J.: Scepter Publishers.

Filas, Francis L., S.J. 1962. *Joseph: The Man Closest to Jesus.* Boston: Daughters of St. Paul.

Friedel, Francis J., S.M. 1928. *The Mariology of Cardinal Newman.* New York: Benziger Brothers.

Friethoff, C. X. J. M., O.P. 1958. *A Complete Mariology.* Trans. "A Religious of the Retreat of the Sacred Heart." London: Blackfriars Publications.

Frossard, André. 1984. *"Be Not Afraid!": Pope John Paul II Speaks Out on His Life, His Beliefs, and His Inspiring Vision for Humanity.* Trans. J. R. Foster. New York: St. Martin's Press.

Johnston, Francis. 1980. *Fatima: The Great Sign.* Rockford, Ill.: Tan Books and Publishers.

_____. 1981. *The Wonder of Guadalupe.* Rockford, Ill.: Tan Books and Publishers.

Jurgens, William A. 1970–79. *The Faith of the Early Fathers.* 3 vols. Collegeville, Minn.: The Liturgical Press.

Kelly, J. N. D. 1960. *Early Christian Doctrines.* 2nd ed. New York: Harper & Row.

_____. 1986. *The Oxford Dictionary of Popes.* Oxford: Oxford University Press.

Llamera, Boniface, O.P. 1962. *Saint Joseph.* Trans. Sr. Mary Elizabeth, O.P. St. Louis: B. Herder Book Co.

McKenzie, John L., S.J. 1965. *Dictionary of the Bible.* New York: The MacMillan Co.

Neuner, J., S.J., and J. Dupuis, S.J. eds. 1990, *The Christian Faith: Doctrinal Documents of the Catholic Church.* Fifth revised and enlarged edition. New York: Alba House.

Newman, John Henry Cardinal. 1949. *Sermons and Discourses (1839–57).* Vol. 2. New York: Longmans, Green and Co.

O'Carroll, Michael, C.S.Sp. 1983. *Theotokos: A Theological Encyclopedia of the Blessed Virgin Mary.* Wilmington, Del.: Michael Glazier.

Our Lady. 1961. Papal teachings selected and arranged by the Benedictine Monks of Solesme. Trans. Daughters of St. Paul. Boston: St. Paul Editions.

Papali, Cyril, O.D.C. 1987. *Mother of God: Mary in Scripture and Tradition.* Chulmleigh, Devon: Augustine Publishing Co.

Parente, Pietro. 1951. *Dictionary of Dogmatic Theology.* First English edition, translated from the second Italian edition by Emmanuel Doronzo, O.M.I. Milwaukee: The Bruce Publishing Co.

Pohle, Joseph, D.D. 1948. *Mariology.* Adapted and edited by Arthur Preuss. St. Louis: B. Herder Book Co.

Ratzinger, Joseph Cardinal. 1983. *Daughter of Zion: Meditations on the Church's Marian Belief.* Trans. John M. McDermott, S.J. San Francisco: Ignatius Press.

Roschini, Gabriel M., O.S.M. 1962. "Mary." *The Marian Era: World Annual of the Queen of the Universe,* vol. 3. Chicago: Franciscan Herald Press.

Scheeben, M. J. 1946–47. *Mariology.* 2 vols. Trans. T. L. M. J. Geukers. St. Louis: B. Herder Book Co.

Smith, George D., D.D. 1938. *Mary's Part in Our Redemption.* New York: P. J. Kenedy & Sons.

Bibliography

Magisterial Texts

Catechism of the Catholic Church.

Congregation for Catholic Education, *The Virgin Mary in Intellectual and Spiritual Formation.*

John Paul II, *Letter of the Holy Father to all the Priests of the Church on the Occasion of Holy Thursday,* 1988: *Mary in the Life of the Priest,* March 25, 1988.

John Paul II, Enc. *Mulieris Dignitatem,* August 15, 1988.

John Paul II, Enc. *Redemptoris Mater,* March 25, 1987.

John Paul II, Apost. Exhort. *Redemptoris Custos,* August 15, 1989.

Leo XIII, Enc. *Magnae Dei Matris,* September 8, 1892.

Leo XIII, Enc. *Augustissimae Virginis,* ASS 30, 129.

National Conference of Catholic Bishops of the United States, *Behold Your Mother: Woman of Faith,* November 21, 1973.

National Conference of Catholic Bishops of the United States, *Collection of Masses of the Blessed Virgin Mary,* Vol. I & II. New York, Catholic Book Publishing Co., 1992.

Our Lady, Papal teachings selected and arranged by the Benedictine Monks of Solesme. Trans. Daughters of St. Paul. Boston, St. Paul Editions, 1961.

Papal Documents on Mary, Ed. by William J. Doheny, C.S.C. & Joseph P. Kelly, S.T.D., Milwaukee, Bruce Publishing Company, 1954.

Paul VI, Enc. *Mense Maio,* April 29, 1965.

Paul VI, Apost. Exhort. *Marialis Cultus,* February 2, 1974.

Paul VI, Apost. Exhort. *Signum Magnum,* May 13, 1967.

Pius IX, Apost. Const. *Ineffabilis Deus,* December 8, 1854.

Pius XI, Enc. *Lux Veritatis*, December 25, 1931.

Pius XII, Apost. Const. *Munificentissimus Deus*, 1950.

Pius XII, Enc. *Fulgens Corona*, September 8, 1953.

Pius XII, Enc. *Ad Caeli Reginam*, October 11, 1954.

Second Vatican Council, Const. *Lumen Gentium*, Chapter Eight, November 21, 1964.

Mary in Scripture

Bojorge S.J., Horacio, *The Image of Mary According to the Evangelists*. Trans. Aloysius Owen SJ, New York, Alba House, 1967.

Braun O.P., *Mother of God's People*. New York, Alba House, 1967.

Buby S.M., Bertrand, *Mary of Galilee, Vol. 1: Mary in the New Testament*. New York, Alba House, 1994.

Buby S.M., Bertrand, *Mary of Galilee, Vol II: Woman of Israel-Daughter of Zion*. New York, Alba House, 1995.

_____, *Mary the Faithful Disciple*. New York, Alba House, 1985.

de la Potterie S.J., Ignace, *Mary in the Mystery of the New Covenant*. Trans. Bertrand Buby S.M., New York, Alba House, 1992.

Deiss C.S.Sp., Lucien, *Mary, Daughter of Sion*. Trans. Barbara T. Blair, Collegeville, The Liturgical Press, 1972.

Feuillet, Andre, *Jesus and His Mother*. Trans. Leonard Maluf, Petersham, St. Bede's Publications, 1973.

Galot S.J., Jean, *Mary and the Gospel*. Trans. Sr. Maria Constance, Westminster, Newman Press, 1965.

Laurentin, Rene, *The Truth of Christmas Beyond the Myths: The Gospel of the Infancy of Christ*. Trans. Michael J. Wrenn, et al., Petersham, St. Bede's Publications, 1982.

Maloney S.D.B., Francis J., *Mary, Woman and Mother*. Collegeville, The Liturgical Press, 1988.

Manelli F.F.I., Stefano M., *All Generations Shall Call Me Blessed: Biblical Mariology*. New Bedford, MA, Academy of the Immaculate, 1995.

Mateo, Fr., *Refuting the Attack on Mary: A Defense of Marian Doctrines*. San Diego, Catholic Answers, 1993.

McHugh, John, *The Mother of Jesus in the New Testament*. New York, Doubleday & Co., Inc., 1975.

Miguens O.F.M., Manuel, *The Virgin Birth: An Evaluation of the Scriptural Evidence*. Westminster, Christian Classics, 1975.

Papali O.D.C., Cyril, *Mother of God: Mary in Scripture and Tradition*. Chulmleigh, Devon, Augustine Publishing Co., 1987.

Mary in Christian Doctrine

Anderson, H. George, Stafford, J. Francis & Burgess, Joseph A. (eds.), *The One Mediator, the Saints and Mary: Lutherans and Catholics in Dialogue VIII*. Minneapolis, Augsburg Press, 1992.

Aquinas, Saint Thomas, *Summa Theologiae*, III, q. 27-30. Trans. Thomas R. Heath, London, Blackfriars, 1969. Vol. LI. (See the Appendix I, "Historical Survey of the Writings of St. Thomas on Our Lady.")

_____, *The Three Greatest Prayers: Commentaries on the Lord's Prayer, the Hail Mary, and the Apostles' Creed*. Trans. Laurence Shapcote O.P. Manchester, N.H.: Sophia Institute, 1990.

Bastero, J. Luis, *Mary, Mother of the Redeemer* (soon to be publishd by Four Courts Press, London.)

Bernard O.P., R., *The Mystery of Mary*. Trans. M.A. Bouchard, St. Louis, B. Herder Book Co., 1960.

Bouyer, Louis, *The Seat of Wisdom: An Essay on the Place of the Virgin Mary in Christian Theology*. Trans. A. Littledale, New York, Pantheon Books, 1962.

Bur, Jacques, *How to Understand the Virgin Mary*. New York, Continuum, 1996.

Carol O.F.M., Juniper B., *Fundamentals of Mariology*. New York, Benziger Brothers, Inc. 1956.

_____, *Mariology*. Milwaukee, The Bruce Publishing Co., 1954.

Friedel S.M., Francis J., *The Mariology of Cardinal Newman*. New York, Benziger Brothers, 1928.

Friethoff O.P., C. X. J. M., *A Complete Mariology*. Trans. "A Religious of the Retreat of the Sacred Heart." London, Blackfriars Publications, 1958.

Frossard, André, *"Be Not Afraid!": Pope John Paul II Speaks Out on His Life, His Beliefs, and His Inspiring Vision for Humanity*. Trans. J. R. Foster. New York, St. Martin's Press, 1984.

Garrigou-LaGrange O.P., Reginald, *The Mother of the Saviour and our Interior Life*. Dublin, Golden Eagle Books Ltd., 1941. (Recently republished by Tan Books.)

Graff, Hilda, *Mary: A History of Doctrine and Devotion*. London, Sheed & Ward, 1963.

Guitton, Jean, *The Virgin Mary*. Trans. A. Gordon Smith, New York, P.J. Kennedy & Sons, 1952

Jelly O.P., Frederick M., *Madonna: Mary in the Catholic Tradition*. Huntingdon, Our Sunday Visitor, 1989.

Johnston, Francis, *Fatima: The Great Sign*. Rockford, Ill., Tan Books and Publishers, 1980.

_____, *The Wonder of Guadalupe*. Rockford, Ill., Tan Books and Publishers, 1981.

Jurgens, William A., *The Faith of the Early Fathers*. 3 vols. Collegeville, The Liturgical Press, 1970–79.

Kelly, J. N. D., *Early Christian Doctrines*. 2nd ed. New York, Harper & Row, 1960.

Laurentin, Rene, *A Short Treatise on the Virgin Mary*. Trans. Charles Neumann S.M., Washington, N.J., AMI Press, 1991.

Maximovitch, St. John, *The Orthodox Veneration of Mary, The Birthgiver of God*. Platina, CA, St. Herman of Alaska Brotherhood, 1994.

McKenzie S.J., John L., *Dictionary of the Bible*. New York: The MacMillan Co., 1965.

Meilach O.F.M, Michael D., *Mary Immaculate in the Divine Plan.* Wilmington, Michael Glazier, Inc., 1981.

Miravalle, Mark I., *Introduction to Mary: the Heart of Marian Doctrine and Devotion.* Santa Barbara, Queenship Publishing, 1993.

Miravalle, Mark I., *Mary: Coredemptrix, Mediatrix, Advocate.* Santa Barbara, Queenship Publishing, 1993.

_____, *Mary: Coredemptrix, Mediatrix, Advocate. Theological Foundations: Toward a Papal Definition (A Collection of Essays on the Topic),* Santa Barbara, Queenship Pubishing, 1995.

Most, William G., *Mary in Our Life.* New York, P.J. Kennedy and Sons, 1954.

_____, *Vatican II: Marian Council.* Dublin, St. Paul Publications, 1972.

Neubert S.M., Emil, *Mary in Doctrine.* Milwaukee, The Bruce Publishing Co., 1954.

Neumann S.M., Charles W., *The Virgin Mary in the Works of St. Ambrose.* Fribourg, The University Press, 1962.

Neuner S.J., J., and J. Dupuis S.J., eds. *The Christian Faith: Doctrinal Documents of the Catholic Church.* Fifth revised and enlarged edition. New York, Alba House, 1990,

O'Carroll S.S.Sp., Michael, *Theotokos: A Theological Encyclopedia of the Blessed Virgin Mary.* Wilmington, Michael Glazier Press, 1982.

Parente, Pietro, *Dictionary of Dogmatic Theology.* First English edition, translated from the second Italian edition by Emmanuel Doronzo, O.M.I. Milwaukee, The Bruce Publishing Co., 1951.

Pohle D.D., Joseph, *Mariology.* Adapted and edited by Arthur Preuss. St. Louis, B. Herder Book Co., 1948.

Prevost, Jean-Pierre, *Mother of Jesus.* Ottawa, Novalis Press, 1988.

Ratzinger, Joseph, *Daughter of Zion.* Trans. John M. McDermott S.J., San Francisco, Ignatius Press, 1977.

Roschini O.S.M., Gabriel M., "Mary." *The Marian Era: World Annual of the Queen of the Universe,* vol. 3. Chicago, Franciscan Herald Press, 1962.

Saward, John, *Redeemer in the Womb*. San Francisco, Ignatius Press, 1993.

Scheeben, M.J., *Mariology*. Trans. Rev. T.L. Geukers, New York, B. Herder Books, 1948.

Schmaus, M., *Dogmatic Theology*, Vol. VIII. Sheed & Ward, 1980.

Suenens, L. J., *Mary the Mother of God*. New York, Hawthorne Books, 1959.

Smith, Canon George D., *Mary's Part in our Redemption*. New York, P.J. Kenedy & Sons, 1954.

Tavard, George H., *The Forthbringer of God: St. Bonaventure on the Virgin Mary*. Chicago, Franciscan Herald Press, 1988.

Tavard, George H., *The Thousand Faces of the Virgin Mary*. Collegeville, The Liturgical Press, 1996.

Vollert S.J., Cyris, *A Theology of Mary*. New York, Herder & Herder, 1965.

Von Balthasar, Hans Urs, *Mary for Today*. San Francisco, Ignatius Press, 1987.

Von Speyr, Adrienne, *The Handmaid of the Lord*. San Francisco, Ignatius Press, 1986.

Mary, the Holy Spirit, and the Church

Baril, Gilberte, *The Feminine Face of the People of God; Biblical Symbols of the Church as Bride and Mother*. Collegeville, The Liturgical Press, 1992.

DeLubac, Henri, *The Motherhood of the Church*. Trans. Sr. Sergian Englund O.C.D., San Francisco, Ignatius Press, 1982.

De Margerie S.J., Bertrand, *Heart of Mary, Heart of the Church*. Trans. Sr. Mary Thomas Noble O.P., Washington, N.J., A.M.I. Press, 1992.

Durrwell, Francois-Xavier, *Mary: Icon of the Spirit and of the Church*. Trans. Robert Nowell, Slough, U.K., St. Paul Publications, 1991.

Hinnebusch O.P., Paul. *Mother of Jesus Present With Us*. Libertyville, Prow Books, 1978.

Jelly O.P., Frederick M. "Discerning the Miraculous: Norms for Judging Apparitions and Private Revelations" in *Marian Studies* XLIV (1993), pp. 41-55.

LaFrance, Jean, *In Prayer with Mary, Mother of Jesus.* Trans. Florestine Audette R.J.M., Sherbrooke, Editions Paulines, 1988.

Miller, Frederick L., *Mary and the Priesthoood.* Washington, N.J., A.M.I Press, 1991.

_____, "The Marian Orientation of Spirituality in the Thought of Pope John Paul II," *Communio,* Winter, 1990.

Philippe O.P., Paul, *The Blessed Virgin and the Priesthood.* Trans. Rev. Laurence J. Spiteri, New York, Alba House, 1993.

Semmelroth S.J., Otto, *Mary Archetype of the Church.* Trans. Maria von Eroes and John Devlin. New York, Sheed & Ward, 1993.

Spiritual Reading for Everyone

Barthas, Casimir, *Our Lady of Light.*

Bernard, Saint, *The Virgin Mother.*

_____, St. Bernard's Sermons on the Blessed Virgin Mary. Trans. from the original Latin by "A Priest of Mount Melleray." Chulmleigh, Devon, Augustine Publishing Co., 1984.

De Montfort, St. Louis-Marie Grignon, *True Devotion to the Blessed Virgin.* Bay Shore, N.Y., Montfort Publications, 1991.

Escrivá, Blessed Josemaría, *Holy Rosary. Christ Passing By (Homilies "To Jesus through Mary," "The Blessed Virgin, Cause of our Joy"). Friends of God (Homily "Mother of God and our Mother").*

Hickey, James Cardinal, *Mary at the Foot of the Cross: Teacher and Example of Holiness.* San Francisco, Ignatius Press, 1988.

Liguouri, Saint Alphonsus, *The Glories of Mary.*

Newman, Cardinal John H., *Mystical Rose* (collection of Marian sermons). Princeton, Scepter, 1997.

_____, *Letter to Pusey.*

_____, *Sermons and Discourses (1839–57)*. Vol. 2. New York, Longmans, Green and Co., 1949.

Perrin, Joseph Marie, *Mary the Mother of Christ and of Christians*.

Sheen, Fulton J., *The World's First Love*, San Francisco, Ignatius Press, 1996.

Suarez, Federico, *Mary of Nazareth*. Princeton, Scepter, 1985.

Walsh, William T., *Our Lady of Fatima*. Doubleday, New York, 1954.

Willam, Franz M., *Mary, My Mother*.

Works on St. Joseph

Filas S.J., Francis L., *Joseph: The Man Closest to Jesus*. Boston, Daughters of St. Paul, 1962.

Llamera O.P., Boniface, *Saint Joseph*. Trans. Sr. Mary Elizabeth, O.P., St. Louis, B. Herder Book Co., 1962.

Suarez, Federico, *Joseph of Nazareth*. Princeton, Scepter, 1984.